S0-FQV-001

PAUL the PHARISEE

North Chapel of Monreale Cathedral, Sicily
Photograph by Sarah Sexton Crossan, July 2015

The Latin inscription reads:

"Paul gives letters to his disciples Timothy and Silas
to be taken through the whole world [*per universum orbem*]."

PAUL the PHARISEE

A Vision Beyond the
Violence of Civilization

John Dominic Crossan

POLEBRIDGE PRESS
Westar Institute, Home of the Jesus Seminar
Salem, Oregon

Scripture quotations, unless otherwise noted, are taken from New Revised Standard Version Bible (NRSV). Copyright © 1989 National Council of the Churches of Christ in the United States of America. Used by permission. All rights reserved.

Copyright © 2024 by John Dominic Crossan

All rights reserved. Printed in the United States of America. No part of this book may be used or reproduced in any manner whatsoever without written permission except in the case of brief quotations embodied in critical articles and reviews.

Polebridge Press is a publishing imprint of the Westar Institute, a non-profit, public-benefit research and educational organization. To learn more about Westar, visit www.westarinstitute.org or contact Westar Publisher: adewey@westarinstitute.org.

Westar Institute, 41877 Enterprise Circle N., Suite. 200,
Temecula, California 92590

Cover design by Sarah Sexton Crossan with Armando Santander
Interior design by Collin Glavac with David Galston

Library of Congress Catalogue-in-Publication Data

Crossan, John Dominic
  Paul the Pharisee: A Vision Beyond the Violence of Civilization
      ISBN   978-1-59815-099-5 (paperback)
  1. Paul--the Apostle, Saint, 2. Paul--the Pharisee, 3. Paul--historical,
  4. Bible N.T.--Luke-Acts, 5. Bible N.T.--Paul and his Vision   I. Title

BS2506.3 C765 2024
227.06—dc23   2023056379

*In memory of Robert W. Funk and the Jesus Seminar
and in celebration of the Westar Institute*

*Thank you to the Polebridge Press team
for your hard work
and dedication to this book:
Art Dewey and David Galston,
Barbara Hampson and Collin Glavac,
Linda Hodges and Armando Santander.*

*Thank you also to Nancy Sexton,
Peoples Printing & Design, Inc.
Clermont, FL*

Contents

Abbreviations

Gen	Genesis
Exod	Exodus
Lev	Leviticus
Num	Numbers
Deut	Deuteronomy
1 Sam	1 Samuel
Isa	Isaiah
Dan	Daniel
Mic	Micah
2 Macc	2 Maccabees
Matt	Matthew
Rom	Romans
1 Cor	1 Corinthians
2 Cor	2 Corinthians
Gal	Galatians
Eph	Ephesians
Phil	Philippians
Col	Colossians
1 Tim	1 Timothy
2 Tim	2 Timothy
1 Pet	1 Peter
Did	*Didache*
JA	*Jewish Antiquities*
JW	*Jewish War*

THE FOURTH MATRIX

Let me now
{ Jolt
Shake and unseat your morticed metaphors.

—Gerard Manley Hopkins, *Yes for a time*

Matrix is a powerful word that comes from the same Greek and Latin roots that give us mother (*mētēr* and *mater*). Matrix is the background you cannot omit—for example, British imperialism to understand Gandhi. Matrix is the context you cannot ignore—for example, American racism to understand King. Matrix is the common sense and general knowledge of any specific time and place—what every-one presumes and understands, be it in acceptance or rejection, about the meanings of its own language and the implications of its own culture. Since we all-too-regularly ignore context and background—especially in biblical interpretation—I prefer a single word like matrix rather than double words like text/context and foreground/back-ground that invite separation, omission, and elimination of those latter terms.

Across my own life, from childhood in Ireland to scholarship in America, from monastic priest to university professor, and from not knowing the Bible at all to knowing it all too well, I am aware of having moved progressively through four successive matrices within which to interpret biblical claims.

That progression would be of minor and secondary interest were it merely my own individual professional development. It is, however, of major and primary interest because that progression has always been in interactive relationship with a succession of commu-nal scholarly matrices for New Testament interpretation. And those themselves have always been in interactive compulsion from contemporary cultural emphases and even political priorities--and not just in America. It is foolish to think that the path you tread is founded by your own steps; that the wave you ride is formed by your own skill; that the wind beneath your wings is fashioned by your own wisdom.

Here, then, are the three cumulative matrices—*Christian, Jewish,* and *Roman*—already established before this present book but leading in it to a fourth or *Evolutionary* matrix within which to conduct an experiment on Paul of Tarsus, Apostle of the Gentiles, and Terror of the New Testament.

The Christian Matrix

I first heard of Paul within a Christian matrix which, *for me,* was not the Evangelical Christianity of America but the Roman Catholicism of Ireland—in the 1930s and 1940s. There, however, Paul was not fully Paul but simply the second and minor component in Saints-Peter-and-Paul. Their feast-day on June 29 was called a "holy day of obligation," that is, if it fell on a weekday, you had to attend Mass and observe it as if it were a Sunday. Still, since it always fell during summer vacation, there was nothing much in it for us when young and at boarding school. In any case, that subordinate status of *PETER-and-paul* did not surprise me as it seemed but another variation on the *HERO-and-sidekick* subservience I already knew so well from the cowboy serials that ran before the main features in our Saturday afternoon movies of the 1940s. As a boy, it was not just Peter-and-Paul or even Peter-and-paul but rather more like PETER'n'paul.

Furthermore, in the wider Christian matrix of Irish Roman Catholicism, I became an altar-boy at the parish church in Naas, County Kildare in 1942. There, as always, the Big Book was not the Christian Bible—had I even heard that word?—but the Roman Missal. Imagine, aged eight, going up and down three altar steps wearing a floor-length soutane carrying that heavy Missal on an equally heavy brass-stand and preferably not dumping that ensemble along the way—especially during Advent when the Big Book was very unequally open.

The Roman Missal did, of course, contain readings from the Old and New Testaments, quotations from the words of Jesus and the letters of Paul, but, extracted in liturgy and included as prayer, nobody ever mentioned biblical literalism. My childhood was salved and my future saved from the fatal fascination of fundamentalism.

Three years later, in 1945, I was enrolled in St. Eunan's College, a boarding high school in Letterkenny, County Donegal, an edifice whose battlemented towers outside were as formidable as its classical curriculum inside. I had Greek and Latin every day for five years and amid the terrors of declensions and conjugations, regular nouns and irregular verbs, I had read Homer in Greek and Virgil in Latin by the time I was sixteen. We had daily Mass, of course, and the Big-Book-Missal was always there but the Big-Book-Bible was still nowhere in sight. Also, unimpeded by the priests who taught us the classics, we unobtrusively adopted our own adolescent skepticism about those Gods and Goddesses stalking the texts of Homer and Virgil. (Some of us were sophisticated enough wags to translate the opening lines of the *Gallic Wars* as: Caesar divided every Gaul into three parts.)

Years later, I recognized and profoundly appreciated the fact that, in Homer, I had read the Old Testament of Roman Imperial Theology and, in Virgil, its New Testament, without knowing it then. Once again, no teacher even opened the question of whether Homer or Virgil should be taken literally or metaphorically. That allowed me, in the fullness of personal time, to read the Christian New Testament and Paul with a similar openness to its literal and/or its metaphorical meaning.

The Jewish Matrix

In 1950, at sixteen, I entered a thirteenth-century Roman Catholic religious order, the Servites, to become a friar—a semi-cloistered monk—as a future missionary in Africa. But, when my superiors looked at my classical résumé, they decided I should be a professor and, after ordination as a priest, they sent me back to Ireland's national seminary at St. Patrick's College in Maynooth, County Kildare, for a doctorate in *Divinity*—the Latin-based equivalent of the Greek-based term *Theology*. Then, immediately, they sent me on to the Jesuit-run Pontifical Biblical Institute, the Biblicum in Rome, for a two-year postdoctoral specialization in biblical exegesis.

Bliss it was in that dawn to be alive / But to be young was very heaven, because Rome, 1959–61, was already preparing for the Second Vatican Council of 1962–65. We priests presumed the Catholic Church *could* change and thought it *would* change—but were wrong on both counts.

By then, of course, I knew the Christian Bible in its Hebrew, Aramaic, and Greek sections, and my New Testament professors were the Jesuit priests Augustin Bea, Maximilian Zerwick, and Stanislaus Lyonnet. It was there and only then that *Peter-and-Paul* moved firmly to become Peter-by-himself and Paul-by-himself, both moving not just within a Christian matrix but within a Jewish one with a Messianic/Christic vision.[1]

For almost an entire year, Father Lyonnet taught a course based on Paul's statement that "just as sin came into the world through one man, and death came through sin, and so death spread to all because all have sinned" (Rom 5:12). But the course focused primarily on a single term in a single part of that single verse in that single epistle. It worked with that terminal "because" or "in whom" (*eph' ho*). Lyonnet argued from Greek but against Latin—Roman!—tradition that *eph' ho* did not indicate an actual genetic but a potential mimetic fault, that Adam had passed on to humanity not an internal sinful state but an external sinful example.

Lyonnet's disruptive interpretation offered sweeping challenges to traditional claims of "original sin" as an innate human inheritance. It negated Augustine's equation of original sin and physical lust, called into question the necessity for infant baptism and therefore the Limbo of unbaptized infants. It negated original sin as inherited by every human child—save for Mary and Jesus who were

---

[1] This is my very deliberately chosen term for Jews who accepted Jesus as the "Messiah"—a word anglicized from the Hebrew or Aramaic—or as the "Christ"—a word anglicized from the Greek. I use that term as both adjective and noun: Paul has a Messianic/Christic vision; Paul is a Messianic/Christic. Later, of course, there would be "Christians" who were non-Jews but, at this early period, the term "Messianic/Christic" is both therapy and prophylaxis.

immaculately conceived without any original fault or sin (Latin *macula*). Furthermore, apart from any private academic course, Lyonnet had already published that interpretation in scholarly journals both at Rome and abroad by the years 1955-56.

In June of 1961, I graduated from the Biblical Institute with a Paul whose Jewish matrix challenged his traditional Christian matrix and that challenge was certified when, in September of 1961, Father Lyonnet—and Father Zerwick—were forbidden by the Vatican from teaching at the Biblicum for the academic year of 1961–62—only to be reinstated by the Second Vatican Council for 1962–63.

That particular Jewish matrix for Paul on original sin as primordial and ancestral bad example was also embedded in an ever widening and deepening consciousness of the general Jewish matrix for Jesus and the entire New Testament during my years at the Biblical Institute.

In 1959. That first fall, I had a course with Father Augustin Bea who came late for class on December 14 when Pope John XXIII made Bea a Cardinal to reconsider ecumenical relations between Judaism and Catholicism in preparation for and participation in the debates and decrees of the forthcoming Council.

In 1960. That summer, with the Summer Olympics arriving at Rome that August-September, I was greatly relieved to be sent by my religious superiors as chaplain to a group of around thirty American pilgrims around the major Catholic shrines or sites in western Europe. We went from Lisbon, Madrid, and Monaco—as a Catholic Shrine with Grace Kelly!—to Italy, Germany and France. That was how, in late August of 1960, I ended up in the Bavarian Alps for the Passion Play at Oberammergau.

As you may know, for deliverance from plague in 1634, the execution of Jesus was vowed by the town to be dramatically represented every ten years. In 1940, however, Bavaria had other concerns, but in 1950, the play returned with Adenauer and Eisenhower in the audience. The play I saw in 1960 was the same version that Hitler saw in 1930 before, and in 1934 after, he became Chancellor of Germany. Here is his infamous review: "It is vital that the Passion Play be continued at Oberammergau; for never has the menace of Jewry been so convincingly portrayed as in this presentation of what happened in the times of the Romans. There one sees in Pontius Pilate a Roman racially and intellectually so superior, that he stands out like a firm, clean rock in the middle of the whole muck and mire of Jewry" (July 5, 1942).

I did, of course, know how the Passion story ended *as text* but when I saw it that day *as drama,* the effect was quietly epiphanic. The play was around six hours long including a good break for lunch and the playhouse had covered seating but was wide open between seating and stage. What struck me forcibly—apart from my being short-sleeved and very cold—was that the play opened on our Palm Sunday with the stage filled by a large crowd all shouting *for* Jesus but closed on our Good Friday with the same crowd all shouting *against* Jesus. The "crowd" had apparently changed its mind about Jesus while we were having lunch and that reversal was never explained *as drama.* The first scholarly article I ever published was about that "crowd" but not just at Oberammergau. Called "Anti-Semitism and the Gospels," it was published, 1965, in the Jesuit journal *Theological Studies,* volume 26, pages 189–214. Understanding correctly the Jewish matrix of the New Testament raised for me this challenge after Oberammergau: how could historical Gospel-research cauterize its theological anti-Judaism from becoming the ongoing seed-bed of racial anti-Semitism?

In 1962. My last step toward formulating for myself the full Jewish matrix of that original Messianic/Christic vision was in the diploma-thesis I prepared under an American visiting professor, Father Francis McCool, S.J. The thesis was that the infancy story of Matthew 1–2 in which an evil ruler tried but failed to kill the chosen child was a literary rewrite of the infancy story of Moses in Exodus 1–2 but filled out by contemporary first-century expansions called *midrashim.* Jesus was the New Moses in parabolic infancy, a promise and prophecy to be fulfilled in his inaugural proclamation of the New Law as the New Moses on the New Mount Sinai in Matthew 5–7.

In summary. Sometimes and very obviously, the Jewish matrix of the New Testament not only backgrounded or expanded the traditional Christian matrix but profoundly challenged its prejudicial discriminations, exegetical illusions, and historical delusions.

The Roman Matrix

In 1965–67 I was sent for another two-year postdoctoral specialization, this time in archaeology, to the Dominican-run *École biblique et archéologique française de Jérusalem*, outside the Damascus Gate of the Old City, then part of the Hashemite Kingdom of Jordan. When I arrived there, I was still an Irish citizen—with two Irish passports. When travelling, I kept one in my left pocket, with every page stamped "Valid for Israel Only"; the other, in the right pocket, was for visas from Syria and Egypt, Iraq and Iran. I was still thinking of specializing in the Old Testament amid Near Eastern imperialism but, after those two years, I was focusing primarily on the New Testament—and Roman imperialism.

I left Jerusalem for a flight—in both senses—from Amman to Rome at dawn on Sunday, June 4, 1967, the day before the Six Day War between Israel and the contiguous Arab States changed everything utterly—there and elsewhere.

Two years later, I left monasticism for marriage and seminary for university. My clerical friends jested that the rescript of laicization had been ready in the Vatican for several years with the fervent hope I might eventually request it. In joining DePaul University in Chicago, I began to study and write about the historical Jesus—with only slight tangential interest in the historical Paul. But while my interest in Jesus has remained constant since 1969, that in Paul came powerfully alive only by the 2000s. And that happened by almost accidental promptings from others.

During two weeks in June of 1999, Jonathan Reed, an archaeologist from the University of La Verne in California who had excavated at Capernaum and Sepphoris, took Sarah and myself to visit major digs from Caesarea Philippi and Jotapata/Yodfat to Qumran and Masada in Israel—places I had not seen in over thirty years. That remedial education prepared me to collaborate with him on our joint book, *Excavating Jesus: Beneath the Stones, Behind the Texts,* published by Harper San Francisco in 2001 and cited among the "Best Religion Books of 2001" by *Publishers Weekly.*

What came next started like a somewhat irreverent joke. Jonathan's brother asked him whether we were going to excavate our way through the main characters in the New Testament, maybe starting with Paul? Jonathan e-mailed me suggesting facetiously that we start on Paul with me at a desk in a library and him on a beach in the Aegean. I replied with equal facetiousness that I would love to excavate Paul but did that mean I would have to read him? But simultaneously with those jokes in the years 1999–2001, something started that forced a radical revision of my understanding of the historical Paul and therefore of the theological Paul.

In that same year, 1999, Canon Marianne Wells Borg, whose Center for Spiritual Development was located at Trinity Episcopal Cathedral in Portland, and her late husband, then Professor Marcus Borg of Oregon State University, invited Sarah and myself to become co-leaders with them on annual journeys with about thirty to forty people "In the Footsteps of Paul." We began in the first two weeks of May 2000 with both Greece and Turkey but decided to focus thereafter on Turkey alone. Also, for cooler weather on the next tour, we moved the date from the first two weeks in May of 2000 to the last two weeks in September 2001. That tour, of course, never happened ...

In the years that followed—from 2002 through 2014—as I read Paul amid the archaeological ruins of the first-century Roman Empire, rather than amid the ideological ruins of the sixteenth-century Reformation, his world, life, history, and theology underwent an absolute sea change for me.

To find Paul's authentic Roman matrix, we visited sites where he had been—from Tarsus through Antioch to Ephesus—but also sites where he never had been—from Priene through Aphrodisias to Ankara. Those latter sites were places where, by the vagaries of preservation, we could glimpse his world ever more accurately. In those annual expeditions, Pauline Messianic Theology came brilliantly alive against Roman Imperial Theology as "the world" of creation against the "this world" of civilization. One immediate result was a second collaboration with Jonathan Reed, *In Search of Paul*, in 2006. For me and forever, Peter-and-paul had passed not to Paul-and-Luther within Reformation polemics but to Jesus-and-Paul within Roman imperialism as first-century Mediterranean globalization.

There was, however, another side to those annual journeys "In Search of Paul" but, although it only surfaced tentatively, it did so with ever-increasing insistence. We were in Turkey primarily and explicitly on a Pauline expedition that secondarily and necessarily involved a Byzantine one. I was thinking of Paul within the eastern Roman Empire, but within both the ruins of its earlier incarnation and the images of its later continuation. For a millennium after the "fall" of the western Roman Empire, Turkey was the homeland of the eastern Roman Empire—called "Byzantium" to obscure and obfuscate that imperial continuity. For me, here is how the earlier Pauline and latter Byzantine world started slowly but surely to coalesce—around the execution and resurrection of Jesus.

On Friday, September 20, 2002, we started in Ankara with the Temple of Rome and Augustus and its *Res Gestae Divi Augusti* as a manifesto of Roman Imperial Theology. After that visit, our expeditionary bus left Ankara for the drive to Tarsus and Antakya—Paul's Antioch on the Orontes River. On the way was Cappadocia where chimneys of volcanic rock were externally carved into strange shapes by tectonic millennia only to be internally carved into homes and monasteries by Byzantine Christians. The Open-Air Museum of Göreme, for example, held a circle of such medieval chapels carved inside volcanic cliffs and although it was all at least a millennium after Paul, it would have been a spiritual and cultural crime not to stop, stay, and wonder.

The crown jewel of Göreme's archaeological park is the Karanlik Kilise or Dark Church, so called because its long unwindowed darkness magnificently preserved this fully frescoed eleventh-century monastic chapel. We stood that day, as always in the Byzantines vision, inside the Christian story as its images whirled all around us and above us. The images—from Nativity through Transfiguration to Crucifixion—were all easily identifiable and completely expected. But then came one that was precisely the opposite. We could see Crucifixion and Ascension but looked in vain for the expected Resurrection. But there was no depiction anywhere of Jesus standing on, hovering over, or ascending from his tomb; no depiction anywhere of cowering soldiers as Jesus resurrected—magnificent, triumphant, but also individual and alone.

Instead we got an utterly divergent image but it was certainly the Resurrection because the Greek term *Anastasis* is inscribed above the head of Jesus. He is shown moving forcibly to viewer-right and treading on the powerful but chained and prostrate figure of Hades-as-Person. The shattered bolts, bars, and locks of Hades-as-Place are scattered all around that Guardian of Death's universal prison house. In his left hand, Jesus holds a cross as symbol of his Crucifixion and both the halo on his head and the shattered double gates of Hades-as-Place at his feet are set in cruciform fashion. With his right hand, Jesus reaches back to grasp the limp wrist of Adam and wrench him from his sepulcher with Eve waiting her turn behind Adam. Again, lest there be any mistake, those twin figures who represent the human race in biblical tradition are clearly named near their heads as "Adam" to his right and "Eve" to her left.

The claim is clear: Resurrection/*Anastasis* means that the Crucified Jesus has liberated the human race from death. Resurrection/*Anastasis* is not the individual liberation of Jesus from death but the universal liberation of humanity with Jesus from the protected prison house of death. But, to put it bluntly, what on earth did that actually mean for our human species? And, of course, you must know what something means before you can either affirm or deny it.

In the following decade, as we returned annually as leaders of a Pauline tour in a Byzantine world, that question became gradually more and more insistent. (We also explored it in private trips before or after the official tour.) In my own evening lectures on tour, I always tried to correlate site and text but, while that was easy in terms of Roman sites and Pauline texts, what about Byzantine *Anastasis*—from the Dark Church in Göreme to the Chora Church in Istanbul—and, say, 1 Cor 15? Would Paul, *mutatis mutandis,* have recognized those images of Jesus' universal Resurrection from Eastern Christianity—rather than those of Jesus' individual Resurrection from western Christianity—as more accurate depictions of what he meant by Christ as "the first fruits of those who have died" (15:20)? In other words, our book, *Resurrecting Easter: How the West Lost and the East Kept the Original Easter Vision,* of 2018, asked that question in preparation for the present book on Paul.

Behind it all, from Jesus and Paul, from Ascension and Resurrection, and from Western and Eastern Christianity, comes this basic question: what, if anything, does Christianity's vision have to do with humanity's evolution? And that leads into the fourth dimension of this book's matrix, into, as it were, the fourth Russian Matryoshka doll which incapsulates those three preceding ones one inside another and—cumulatively—within itself.

The Evolutionary Matrix

You will soon see that books by three European philosophers— (the late) Jacob Taubes from Germany, Alain Badiou from France, and Giorgio Agamben from Italy—are cited as chapter epigraphs[2] throughout this book. By treating Paul as a philosopher, they accept the validity of discussing his modern relevance. That question of current relevance applies to all thinkers claiming to speak across time and space for humanity, the world, the earth, the universe. Such claims may well be accepted or rejected, muted or modified but, if given as declared authorial vision, intended literary purpose, and dedicated rhetorical strategy, they should at least be acknowledged and judged accordingly. A Plato should not be discussed as speaking only or even primarily to ancient Greeks. A Paul should not be discussed as speaking only or even primarily to ancient Gentiles. They claimed to speak across time and place and should be assessed on that claim. Also, I would add, as philosophers cannot skip Socrates in Plato, philosophers cannot skip Jesus in Paul.

It is certainly correct, for example, to see Paul—as those philosophers do—in opposition to Roman imperialism in its ancient or modern incarnations. Still, Rome was but the normalcy of civilization in first-century time, Mediterranean place, and toga dress. Paul's problem, therefore, was civilization itself and his challenge was to imagine and incarnate post-civilization. That is still our problem as the earth's most endangered because most endangering species. For me, therefore, it is the normalcy of civilization that presses beyond philosophical not to theological but to evolutionary thought—with regard to contemporary Pauline relevance.

---

[2] For full details on any epigraph, see the *Works Consulted* on page 199.

Our particular species, named *Homo sapiens* with ineffable irony, left Africa at least seventy thousand years ago by land passage northward on the Levantine coastline or by sea passage eastward on the Arabian coastline. Then, in effect, even if not in design, the *bitter* angels of our nature declared an integrated threefold onslaught on the world: on the physical environment resulting now in ever-accelerating climate change; on all other species resulting now in ever-accelerating biodiversity loss; and on ourselves resulting now in ever-accelerating weapons of mass destruction. We endanger ourselves atomically, biologically, chemically, demographically, ecologically—and are only up to *e* in our apocalyptic alphabet. This is the Holocene as Hollowscene, the Anthropocene as Anthropocide, the world as *Titanic* and we its iceberg.

The biblical tradition was primarily or even exclusively aware of that last onslaught on one another with weapons of war. It longed for divine and human cooperation in "days to come" when *God* "shall judge between the nations, and arbitrate for many peoples" and *"they* shall beat their swords into plowshares, and *their* spears into pruning hooks; nation shall not lift up sword against nation, neither shall *they* learn war any more" (Isa 2:2–4=Mic 4:1–3). That anvil chorus is still awaited in blessed hope but now we already know what the biblical tradition could never have imagined: that a day would come *and now is* when the environmental legacy of plowshare and pruning hook would be at least as dangerous as the martial heritage of sword and spear.

The result from that triple onslaught is that human violence is not just an ethical problem about the responsibility of our actions, be it theological or philosophical, but an evolutionary problem about the sustainability of our species. The divinity behind Dante and Brueghel may be greeted with *fear-nots* but the humanity behind Dachau and Buchenwald must be greeted with *fear-lots*.

Granted that fullest matrix, my purpose in this book is to conduct an experiment on Paul within that fourth or *Evolutionary* matrix as, of course, the cumulative climax of those other three. What does Paul's vision of our world have to do—or does it have anything to do—with human evolution within cosmic evolution? What would ancient Paul look like and sound like if seen through a modern evolutionary understanding of the universe?

Can Paul speak in the public sphere to those who never were religious or are now areligious or even anti-religious? Beneath the peculiarities of his own language and rhetoric or behind the particularities of his own time and place, does Paul have any visionary wisdom to console, inspire, and direct us into our future? What, in any case, is the enabling passion, constitutive intuition, and generative vision that inflames Paul's imagination and drives Paul's mission? Also, does it translate from then to now?

Furthermore, I can think immediately of three objections, any of which might kill this book at birth. So here, at least initially, is how I would respond to them.

First, about God. Paul's visionary challenge was founded by and grounded in a Supreme Being—the Big God as Person—whose Creation works by divine punishments negated by forgiveness or mitigated by mercy. What happens when such a God is now no longer credible to so many of us?

There is still and always the Supremacy of Being—the Big Bang as Mystery—whose Creation works not by divine punishments but by evolutionary consequences which are humanly processed not by forgiveness but by our ability to change and mitigated not by mercy but by the time given before change is too late. If external divine punishments, forgiveness, and mercy are not credible, then internal evolutionary consequence, change, and time still are—and always were. (I distinguish punishment from consequence like this: drunk driver hits tree and is fined by police—that comes externally as punishment; drunk driver hits tree and is killed by crash—that comes internally as consequence.) Thus, with all due respect for President Lincoln, it was not as divine punishment but as human consequence that "every drop of blood drawn with the lash shall be paid by another drawn with the sword."

Second, about Metaphor. Paul's Judeo-*Pharisaic* vision of a Supreme Being who, at end-time, will finally establish cosmic justification through the triple interlock of universal resurrection for general judgment with consequent eternal recompense for all humanity is incredible to the point of absurdity. Yes, if taken literally but what if taken metaphorically? What if it is a parable of human responsibility and human accountability. As end-time singularity becomes in-time regularity, Paul's Pharisaic vision is a powerfully persuasive cost-accounting for the war of our species, *Homo sapiens,* on our environment, on all other species, and on ourselves.

Finally, about Time. At least initially, Paul thought that the climax and consummation of cosmic resurrection-judgment-sanctions would occur within his own lifetime. He spoke of *"we* who are alive, who are left until the coming of the Lord . . . *we* who are alive, who are left" (1 Thess 4:15,17); "I mean, brothers and sisters, the appointed time has grown short'" (1 Cor 7:19); and *"we* will all be changed . . . *we* will be changed" (1 Cor 15:51–52). Even in his last letter: "you know what time it is . . . salvation is nearer to us now than when we became believers" (Rom 13:11).

Paul, like so much of the New Testament, was flatly wrong that time would *soon* come to some divine termination (So, also, was Jesus wrong, if he—and not those writing in his name—said the same?) Does that partially or totally invalidate Paul's message? Does a mistake about its ending invalidate the importance of a happening? In fact, might a debate about an ending be a calculated flight from the challenge of a starting?

As the wider promulgation of Jesus' message, Paul's was not just a message about future time, but a challenge about present time. It was a message about participating in what must happen rather than about speculating about when it might end. Paul thought that end would be soon. He was completely wrong. So, if your time is wrong, can your message still be valid? Yes, and that is why Paul's message survived. It was fully experienced as a correct present-already life commitment by enough followers to render irrelevant any claim about an incorrect future-soon consummation.

They told a parable. To what is the matter like? It is like an epidemic which strikes two adjacent countries. One ruler mandates face masks for all and says that the threat will pass in a month. The other ruler dismisses face masks for anyone and says that the threat will pass in a year. The first ruler was wrong on time but his message saved a million lives. The second ruler was right on time but his message cost a million lives.

Chapter 1

A TALE OF TWO METAPHORS

Now it happens that the Jewish study of Paul is in a very sad state. There is a literary corpus about Jesus, a nice guy, about the rabbi in Galilee . . . But when it comes to Paul, there's a borderline that's hard to cross. . . . This is the point at which little Jacob Taubes comes along and enters into the business of gathering the heretic back into the fold. I regard him—this is my own personal business—as more Jewish than any Reform rabbi, or any Liberal rabbi, I ever heard in Germany, England, America, Switzerland, or anywhere.

—Jacob Taubes, *The Political Theology of Paul*

On the morning of September 23, 31 BCE, the three squadrons of Octavian's battle-fleet emerged from Greece's Ambracian Gulf, cleared Cape Actium, and formed up in line abreast to face Anthony's threesome in the open Ionian Sea. Cleopatra's single squadron came out behind Antony's central one but her flagship, with treasure chest and sails on board, was set for flight not fight. In the afternoon, as the wind shifted to the northwest and the battle lines opened up, she picked up Antony, swept through Octavian's lines, rounded the shoulder of Leukas island, and sailed to Alexandria for immortality in history, legend, and gossip. After twenty years of savage on-again off-again civil war, Octavian was now *Princeps,* first among equals with all the equals dead.

Less than a year later, on August 1, 30 BCE, Octavian—the soon-to-be Augustus—entered Alexandria as conqueror of Egypt. Within two weeks, both Antony and Cleopatra were dead and Octavian had to think about Cleopatra's four Roman children. Cleopatra and Julius Caesar had a son, named Caesarion (Little Caesar). Cleopatra and Marc Antony first had twins named for sun and moon as

Alexander Helios and Cleopatra Selene, then another child named Ptolemy Philadelphus. Would the child by Caesar, the Roman general who had adopted him, receive better treatment from Octavian than the children by Antony, the Roman general who had opposed him? Exactly the opposite.

Octavian sent Antony's three children to be reared at Rome in the household of his own elder sister Octavia who had become Antony's wife in 40 BCE even as Antony was starting that family with Cleopatra! Octavia was legendary for virtue and that must surely have included supreme tolerance, ineffable patience, and awesome restraint. That left Octavian with the problem of Caesarion who was, after his parents' double suicide, Ptolemy XV Caesar, Pharaoh of Egypt, and a problem not just literal and political but metaphorical and theological.

Octavian's proper name was not that diminutive nickname Octavian (Little Octavius) but Gaius Julius Caesar Octavius since he had been adopted as son and also heir in the will of his grand-uncle, the assassinated and then deified Julius Caesar. That made him, as his Latin inscriptions proclaimed, *Divi Filius* or Son of the Divine One, and as his Greek ones announced, *Theou Huios*, Son of God. But Octavian was the adopted Son of the Divine Julius Caesar while Caesarion was the conceived Son. Here then is the final question: did Octavian take his own and Caesarion's divinity literally or metaphorically when he sent the stranglers to assassinate Caesarion that late March of 30 BCE? Or, as he saw them approach, did that seventeen-year-old teenager stutter plaintively that he was only a metaphor?

On the situation of Octavian and Caesarion, I have never been asked about the literal or metaphorical understanding of divinity. But on Jesus and Paul, that question almost always comes up in question time after lectures. Granted, someone will ask, that *you* take Paul's "Son of God" for Jesus metaphorically, did *Paul* himself take it literally? The inference is that the literal is what must be taken *seriously* and the alternative—with overt or covert qualifications—is just a metaphor, simply a metaphor, merely a metaphor, and basically irrelevant. It is time, therefore, to think seriously about metaphor.

We are aware in general of the minor metaphors we make but oblivious to the major ones that make us. In "The Promising," from his 1963 book, *A Sky of Late Summer,* the poet Henry Rago imagined "The metaphor not means but end / Not the technique / But the vocation the destiny." But vocation and destiny are not just for poetry sometimes but for humanity always. Because: a lived-out metaphor is how our species creates its reality—for good or bad; a lived-out metaphor is how we create our world—for life or death.

We recognize that a metaphor such as "clouds sail across the sky" carries across—from Greek *meta*/across and *pherein*/to carry—the attributes of one phenomenon or situation to another one. Metaphor involves seeing-as and, in that example, seeing-skies-as-seas and seeing-clouds-as-sails were originally valid conceits but eventually vapid clichés. That is all quite clear and you may well yawn as you read it. After all, the components of both sea-scape and sky-scape are quite visible to our eyes already. But what if someone were standing by the Nile millennia ago, watching the clouds move across the sky, and imagining what was not yet existent—sailing—and inventing what was not yet named—boating? What if metaphor is the only way for inventing human reality by carrying-over from the non-existent to the existent?

When we get to the great political mega-metaphors—like autocracy, oligarchy, or democracy—or the great religious ones—like atheism, polytheism, or monotheism—that create human reality when lived out communally, we forget that reality is always lived metaphor, that humanity has no exit strategy from metaphoricity, and that metaphor still needs to be regularly jolted, continually shaken, and periodically unseated—because of the dynamic cosmic evolution within which we live, move, and have our being.

In summary. The seeing-as of metaphor is not just rhetorical flourish or poetic gesture but human necessity and species-based inevitability. You may prefer "sun's up" to *Hamlet's* "But look, the morn, in russet mantle clad, / Walks o'er the dew of yon high eastward hill" but the metaphors that create our poetry are but elegant miniatures of those that create our reality—but also gossamer warnings of metaphor's foundational inevitability for our species. As Shakespeare's Prospero might have said: *We have such dreams as stuff is made on.*

Think, for example, of these two cases of *seeing-as* from the early 1930s: one was Roosevelt's "New Deal," the other Hitler's "Thousand-Year Reich." When those metaphors were lived out communally, each created its own human reality—for good or evil, life or death. Or think today of seeing-as in the competing metaphors of capitalism—the Russian criminal one, the Chinese autocratic one, and the American legal one—and think how each one imports elements of the other two. Those three metaphors create reality for most of our present-day world and one of them or some alternative to all of them will be our future. But. whatever will be, will be a metaphor lived into a reality that works for us only when and if human evolution tracks and changes in conformity with cosmic evolution.

As I prepare to turn from that general overture on metaphor to the two particular metaphors that ground this book, here are two points as a transition.

First, the innate problem of our species is not original sin but original state. We are a social species with individual wills. Our species sustainability as *Homo sapiens* presumes we are *sapiens* enough to reject an individualism ever lured toward anarchy and/or a universalism ever lured toward tyranny. Watch, therefore, for the rest of this chapter and this book, that species-wide fault line between the individual-personal and the social-universal.

Second, there were two profoundly different mega-metaphors available for consummating human reality—and thereby creating its back-story—at the start of the Common Era's first century in antiquity. They were, I repeat, radically divergent from one another but also equally grounded along that just-mentioned fault line between the individual and the universal that both constitutes the identity of our species but also challenges its sustainability.

Ascension

The first and older metaphor was not found exclusively in Jewish culture but was commonly and transculturally available in Jewish, Greek, and Latin worlds as part of the Mediterranean wallpaper.

Ascension meant that, apart from the masses who *descended* ultimately to oblivion in Jewish Sheol or Greco-Roman Hades, certain privileged individuals were assumed at death into heavenly life and immortal memory with God or the Gods. For the human protagonist that was *ascension—apotheōsis* in Greek, *deificatio* in Latin, *divinization* in English.

Here is the job description for a human's ascension to divinity: the candidate must have established some extraordinary benefit for humanity here below and thereby manifested some particular aspect of divinity there above. Such ascension was always individual and personal but never secret or private. In written text and marble statue, immortal personal life meant immortal public memory. Such an ascendancy was applicable to a saint in Judaism or a hero in Romanism but, in that first century, it was internationally, transculturally, and especially applicable to religio-political founders—like the Jewish Moses or the Roman Romulus.

Moses would seem an improbable candidate for ascension to God or assumption by God because of the biblical account of his death and burial:

> Moses, the servant of the Lord, died there in the land of Moab, at the Lord's command. He was buried in a valley in the land of Moab, opposite Beth-peor, but no one knows his burial place to this day. (Deut 34:5–6)

It was, however, the final "no one knows his burial place" that opened up a possibility apparently closed by the preceding diptych of "died . . . was buried."

First, according to Josephus,[1] during Moses' long absence alone with God atop Mount Sinai, some of the waiting Israelites thought that he had "fallen a victim of wild beasts" but "others that he had been taken back to the divinity . . . and that he should be translated by God to Himself by reason of his inherent virtue was likely enough" (*JA* 3.96–97).

Next, with that preparation, Josephus is ready to retell the biblical account of the death and burial of Moses:

---

[1] Quotations of Josephus are from *Josephus*. Vols. I-X. Trans. by H. St. J. Thackeray, Ralph Marcus, & Louis H. Feldman. Loeb Classical Library. Cambridge, MA: Harvard University Press, 1966-1981.

> While he bade farewell to Eleazar and Joshua and was yet communing with them, a cloud of a sudden descended upon him and he disappeared in a ravine. But he has written of himself in the sacred book that he died, for fear lest they should venture to say that by reason of his surpassing virtue he had gone back to the Divinity. (*JA* 4.326)

That passage both acknowledges that Moses "died" in the biblical account and negates it by the heavenly cloud and earthly disappearance.

Finally, when Philo[2] describes what happened to Moses he uses a similar admission-and-negation device to translate the biblical tradition into ascension/assumption. At the moment,

> when he was about to depart from hence to heaven, to take up his abode there, and leaving this mortal life to become immortal, having been summoned by the Father . . . when he was now on the point of being taken away, and was standing at the very starting-place, as it were, that he might fly away and complete his journey to heaven. (*On the Life of Moses* 2.288,291)

In fact, Moses *foretold* how he would be buried "without anyone being present so as to know his tomb, because in fact he was entombed not by mortal hands, but by immortal powers" (2.291).

For both Josephus and Philo, despite the biblical account of Moses' death and burial, the biblical admission that his tomb was unknown allowed the claim of his ascension to God in assumption by God.

Romulus moves far beyond that rather simple case of Moses. His ascension is confirmed by an apparition that included prophetic message and visionary mandate.

---

[2] Quotations of "Life of Moses" are from *The Works of Philo*. Complete and Unabridged. New Updated Edition. Trans. by C. D. Yonge. Peabody, MA: Hendrickson Publishers, 1993; quotations of "Every Good Man is Free" and "The Special Laws" are from *Philo*. Vols. I-X. Trans. F. H. Colson. Loeb Classical Library. Cambridge, MA: Harvard University Press, 1941-1997.

First, all four authors[3] agree that Romulus' death involved his disappearance during an unusual daytime darkness: "sudden darkness . . . out of a clear sky and a violent storm" (Dionysius); "a violent thunderstorm suddenly arose . . . a dense cloud" (Livy); Jupiter "veiling the sky with dark clouds . . . thunder and lightning" (Ovid); "the light of the sun failed, and night came down . . . with awful peals of thunder and furious blasts driving rain from every quarter" (Plutarch).

Next, all four agree that one explanation of Romulus' sudden disappearance was his ascension: He was "caught up into heaven by his father Mars" (Dionysius); "he had been snatched away to heaven by a whirlwind" (Livy); Mars "raising him from earth set him in heaven" (Ovid); "he had been caught up into heaven, and was to be a benevolent god for them instead of a good king" (Plutarch).

There was, however, another explanation for Romulus' disappearance—not ascension but assassination. In that alternative version, Romulus had been murdered by the patrician senators and his body dismembered to be secretly removed under their cloaks (Dionysius, Livy, and Plutarch).

Then, presumably to scotch that murderous version, two authors confirm ascension over assassination by citing an apparition to a very important and trustworthy senator named Proclus. He proclaimed solemnly that: "at break of dawn, to-day, the Father of this City suddenly descended from heaven and appeared to me" (Livy); or that "as he was travelling on the road, he had seen Romulus coming to meet him, fair and stately to the eye as never before and arrayed in bright and shining armor" (Plutarch).

Finally, both those latter authors confirm ascension even further by having Romulus' apparition give Proclus a visionary mandate for the Roman people: so that "no human might can withstand the arms of Rome" (Livy); or so that "Romans . . . will reach the utmost heights of human power" (Plutarch).

---

[3] The four main sources are on the internet: Dionysius of Halicarnassus (60–67 BCE), *Roman Antiquities* 2.56; Livy (59 BCE–12 CE), *History of Rome* 1.16; Ovid (43 BCE–17 CE), *Metamorphoses* 14.805–28; and Plutarch (46–119 CE), *Life of Romulus* 27.3–28.3. All can be accessed under "Greek and Roman Materials" at: https://www.perseus.tufts.edu.

In summary. By the first century CE, the metaphor of *ascension* (Greek: *apotheōsis*) involved four aspects. It indicated individual exaltation, personal glory, and immortal memory; it only applied to individuals deemed of extraordinary merit who thereby revealed some facet of divinity; it was a possibility accepted cross-culturally by both Jewish and Greco-Roman traditions; it was permanently available at any time and any place.

Augustus, for example, died and was cremated in 14 CE and ascended into heaven among the Gods; for the Jewish philosopher Philo: "the rest of the habitable world had decreed him honors equal to those of the Olympian gods" (*Embassy to Gaius* 149); and for the Roman historian Suetonius: "there was even an ex-praetor who took oath that he had seen the form of the Emperor [Augustus], after he had been reduced to ashes, on its way to heaven" (*The Deified Augustus* 94.4). *Ascension* was alive and well cross-culturally in the world of Jesus—and is, of course, *mutatis mutandis,* still alive and well in contemporary fantasies about Super Heroes who never die and modern delusions about Super Leaders who never lose.

Resurrection

The second and newer metaphor was exclusively Jewish but even there it was restricted to a sectarian one within the Pharisaic tradition. When did belief in resurrection arrive within Judaism, what did it entail, why did it arrive there so late, and how did it differ so radically from *ascension?*

For almost the entire biblical tradition, divine retributive justice was believed to operate according to deuteronomic theology with rewards "if you will only obey the Lord your God" and punishments "if you will not obey the Lord your God" (Deut 28: 1, 15). Those sanctions worked for or against Israel's fertility, prosperity, security, and victory but always in this life, within this world, upon this earth here below. Afterward, there was only Sheol as the dust, gloom, and darkness of the Grave writ large. There was no afterlife in any meaningful sense—as there was most visibly in adjacent Egypt. (And, of course, Israel knew all about Egypt but probably considered its claims for human immortality a typical piece of pagan impertinence.)

But, then, in the middle of the 160s BCE Israel's belief in human lives and divine sanctions as only fulfilled here below changed completely—at least for some—like this.

In Syria, the successor empire of the dead Alexander was ruled by Antiochus IV Epiphanes but he was squeezed of old by Egypt from the south and anew by Rome from the west. To consolidate his tottering empire, Antiochus IV decided to force recalcitrant Israel into close socio-economic and tight religio-political subjection. Among those who refused to apostatize were both the Maccabean militants who fought him, won, and thereby certified the power of God, as well as the Maccabean martyrs who refused him, died, and thereby questioned the justice of God.

The theological questions were inevitable: where was divine justice for the bruised, battered, brutalized bodies of those martyrs? How did the deuteronomic theology of divine justice work for them? The theological answers were immediate: divine justice was not revealed here but hereafter, not in this world but in the next, not by ascension but by resurrection. That invention claimed that, at the end of time, there would be, there had to be, a universal resurrection of the dead, a general judgment on them all, and subsequent rewards in heaven or punishments in hell. The deuteronomic theology was alive and well, possibly here but certainly hereafter, possibly sooner but certainly later—and not just for souls but for bodies.

Note: Resurrection is never individual but always universal; Resurrection is always a shorthand term for that triadic process of universal resurrection for general judgment and subsequent sanctions. Also, of course, it is a double metaphor of exaltation for some and retribution for others—and each aspect may be presented with equal emphasis or one with more emphasis than the other.

First, there is a hint of all this in the book of Daniel from the 160s BCE. You can see the shift from sanctions in this life to sanctions in the next life as the stories in Daniel 1–6 cede place to the visions in Daniel 7–12. In the former half of that book, the Three Youths in the Fiery Furnace (3:1–30) and Daniel in the Lions' Den (6:1–28) are all rewarded by divine deliverance before death. But, in the latter half of the book, there is this promise of divine deliverance after death: "Many of those who sleep in the dust of the earth shall awake, some to everlasting life, and some to shame and everlasting contempt. Those who are wise shall shine like the brightness of the sky, and those who lead many to righteousness, like the stars forever and ever" (12:2–3). Reward, deliverance, salvation from death came not before death but after death—by and within the "resurrection of the dead ones."

Next, by 100 BCE, the clearest manifesto for life-after-death sanctions is in the story of the Mother with Seven Sons (2 Macc 7). Faced with bodily torture and death if they would not reject ancient Judaism for modern Hellenism, the sons accept their present martyrdom in assurance of their future bodily resurrection and, finally, that is confirmed by their mother:

> The King of the universe will raise us up *(anastēsei)* to an everlasting renewal of life, because we have died for his laws.
>
> I got these [limbs] from Heaven, and because of his laws I disdain them, and from him I hope to get them back again.
>
> One cannot but choose to die at the hands of mortals and to cherish the hope God gives of being raised again *(anastēsesthai)* by him. But for you there will be no resurrection *(anastasis)* to life!
>
> The Creator of the world, who shaped the beginning of humankind and devised the origin of all things, will in his mercy give life and breath back to you again, since you now forget yourselves for the sake of his laws. (7:9,11,14,23)

Notice the Greek terms used for the noun "resurrection" *(anastasis)* and the verb "to raise up" *(anistēmi)*. Also, since they suffered *bodily* tortures here, there had to be *bodily* recompenses hereafter. But, above all else, what was at stake was whether the world was or was not ruled by divine cosmic justice: *resurrection* was for universal *judgment,* and universal *judgment* was for universal *recompense.*

Finally, by 100 CE, the appropriate recompense for good or evil was spelled out as an appropriate *location* of reward or punishment:

The earth shall give up those who are asleep in it; and the chambers shall give up the souls which have been committed to them. And the Most High shall be revealed upon the seat of judgment, and compassion shall pass away, and faithfulness shall grow strong. And recompense shall follow, and the reward shall be manifested; righteous deeds shall awake, and unrighteous deeds shall not sleep. Then the pit of torment shall appear and opposite it shall be the place of rest; and the furnace of Hell shall be disclosed, and opposite it the Paradise of delight. (4 Ezra 7:32–36)

That is the full scenario of divine cosmic justice as a climactic end-time product: resurrection, judgment, sanctions in heaven or hell—for all who have ever lived. Let me repeat that the term "resurrection" was but the first-step shorthand for that entire three-step product. It was always and ever about divine justice manifested—remedially?—on a universal and cosmic scale.

Here, in summary, are the multiple differences between those two metaphors as options with which to consummate a world of reality at the start of the first common-era century. I place them side-by-side to make their differences as obvious as possible:

Table 1

The Metaphor of Ascension (Greek: *Apotheōsis*)	*The Metaphor of Resurrection* (Greek: *Anastasis*)
is a metaphor of individual exaltation,	is a metaphor of universal justification,
of ultimate personal glory,	of ultimate cosmic justice,
and of memorial *immortality* for self	and of immemorial *responsibility* for world
accepted cross-culturally within both Jewish and Greco-Roman traditions	accepted as a sectarian reality only within Jewish-Pharisaic tradition
by the first century CE	by the first century CE
as a permanent possibility of in-time	as an ultimate possibility of end-time

—· ·· ·····❖····· ·· —

We may debate whether those two concepts were taken literally or metaphorically in the past or which way they should be taken—if taken at all rather than dismissed derisively—in the present. We may also wonder whether the sectarian Jewish concept of Resurrection was confused with or even collapsed into the cross-cultural Mediterranean concept of Ascension. But all such discussions should arise only after their radical divergence is understood.

I conclude this chapter with questions. Those metaphors of Ascension and Resurrection arose within the matrix of God and Religion, Bible and Christianity, Jesus and Paul. What if somebody is absolutely uninterested in or actively opposed to that ancient matrix? What if somebody finds antiquity's metaphors about individual ascension to God or universal justification by God simply irrelevant to modernity? What if, conversely, somebody takes those metaphors literally and, trapped in affirming or negating them as such, never even hears their abiding challenge?

My own interpretive location is where two vectors intersect or twin matrices meet: one, just seen, is the tradition of biblical experience; the other is the trajectory of human evolution. But those two vectors of Bible and Evolution are not independent ones. The integrity and validity of the biblical tradition depends absolutely on whether and to what extent it tracks closely with human evolution within cosmic evolution. The repeated fall of empires in Daniel 2 or 7 can, for example, be accepted or rejected as punishments from the retributive justice of God. But any negation of God's external punishments cannot exempt us from evolution's internal consequences.

The tectonic plates moving inexorably beneath us now did not wait for us to arrive and did not care about any delay in our advent. Cosmic evolution does not worry if we do not recognize its supremacy. Human evolution does not worry if we do not acknowledge its ascendancy. Evolution was always there and operative whether we knew it or not and whether we accepted it or not. Maybe religions are ritualized intimations of evolution, theologies are odes to evolution seen through a glass darkly.

Here are this book's questions to those for whom the biblical tradition is dead and gone. Are we, like the saber-toothed tiger, a magnificent but doomed species? Is, once again, our tragic flaw not original sin but original state, that is, our evolutionary status as a social species with individual wills? To reconcile that dichotomy, we do not have automatic instinct but only moral conscience, that "knowledge of good and evil" with which we staggered out of Eden to face our destiny and confront the dichotomy of our nature. Does our species, therefore, have a sustainable existence or a fatal genetic disjunction?

What if we relocate Ascension and Resurrection from the biblical to the evolutionary matrix? Do you think it makes a difference to live by the ascension metaphor of special privilege on the personal and individual level or by the resurrection metaphor of cosmic responsibility on the communal and universal level? Those are both metaphors, of course, but they are different ones and therefore create different realities when we live by one, by the other, or by their reconciliation. And, of course, their only alternative is some other metaphor by which to live and create our reality.

Our species has an ongoing trajectory of escalatory violence against the environment, other species, and ourselves. In that situation, the sustainability of *Homo sapiens* may make it rigorously necessary to believe in that metaphor of cosmic responsibility and global accountability and act accordingly before it is too late. To repeat: disbelief about extrinsic divine punishments at end-time does not excuse us from belief about intrinsic evolutionary consequences as end-time. That is why we can read Paul bilingually: within the biblical challenge for Christianity's legacy and/or within the evolutionary challenge for humanity's destiny.

Granted that understanding, here are more questions on either side of that and/or. Were both metaphors, Ascension and Resurrection, there for the interpretation of Jesus' crucifixion from the beginning? Were they both equally present from, as it were, that first Easter Sunday morning? Or did the original and earlier interpretation of Jesus' death assert his Ascension—which only morphed into his Resurrection later? If so, when and how did that change occur? Did it come exclusively or primarily from Paul as a Messianic/Christic

Pharisee? Before Paul, do we have *any* certain mention of Jesus' Resurrection as distinct from his Ascension? In the pre-Pauline hymn of Phil 2:6–11, Jesus was "highly exalted (*hyper-ypsōsen*)" and, in the prePauline creed of 1 Cor 15:3b–7, Jesus was "raised up (*egēgertai*) on the third day." Are those secure references to Universal Resurrection rather than to Individual Ascension?

Chapter 2

THE QUESTION OF DUE DILIGENCE

> Why invoke and analyze this fable? Let us be perfectly clear:
> so far as we are concerned, what we are dealing with here is
> precisely a fable. And singularly so in the case of Paul, who
> for crucial reasons reduces Christianity to a single statement:
> Jesus is resurrected. . . . Let us say that so far as we are con-
> cerned it is rigorously impossible to believe in the resurrection
> of the crucified.
>
> —Alain Badiou, *Saint Paul: The Foundation of Universalism*

Biblical scholars have always used "source criticism" as part of the
integrity of historical research but now that obligation has moved far,
far beyond an academic discipline. We now live—verbally and visu-
ally, nationally and internationally—in a world of smiling lies, alternative facts, fake news, aspirations masquerading as interpretations,
and conspiracy theories where truth is at best a personal opinion or
at worst an obsolete artifact. (But, of course, logic mocks the claim
that there is no truth—can you hear its laughter?)

It is necessary now more than ever to defend the very possibility of truth and call things by their proper name—in politics and
religion, public square and church sanctuary. To do so requires, to use
juridical terms, due diligence, fiduciary obligation, and source criticism. Here, for example, is how *Wikipedia* defines that term today
and the application goes far beyond biblical criticism:

> **Source criticism** (or **information evaluation**) is the
> process of evaluating an information source, i.e. a doc-
> ument, a person, a speech, a fingerprint, a photo, an
> observation, or anything used in order to obtain knowl-
> edge. In relation to a given purpose, a given information

source may be more or less valid, reliable or relevant. Broadly, "source criticism" is the interdisciplinary study of how information sources are evaluated for given tasks.

As sources, biblical texts are not exempt from such evaluation. Rather, since their authors invoke transcendental authority to make universal claims, they should be subject to the most careful scrutiny and critical appraisal—especially with regard to sources for information and to authorial intentions in such sources. (Opinion without evidence is bias; opinion against evidence is prejudice.)

This book's due diligence began with the preceding chapter's foundational distinction between two ancient metaphors for human exaltation, two interpretations for understanding, say, an emptied tomb or a visionary experience, two options, therefore, already available within their contemporary world for those proclaiming the vindication of the executed Jesus.

One preliminary point, since we all speak so easily about the *Gospels* in the plural. The Greek word *eu/aggelion* means a *good/message* or *good/news* or *gospel* (singular). In the New Testament, there is only one Gospel, namely, the Good News of Jesus as the Messiah/Christ in vision and mission, in life and death. But to cite any news as good (or bad), is to make and claim an interpretation. Furthermore, the New Testament itself offers us four such interpretations which it openly, clearly, and honestly calls four "according to"s. I turn first to two such interpretations of that single Good News that were even earlier than the canonical foursome and rather surprising in comparison with one another.

The Gospel according to Q

In terms of its discovery, this gospel-version had been hiding in plain sight for almost two thousand years until it was finally discovered and named in German biblical scholarship by 1900, and that given name has stuck ever since. First, scholars noticed that the similarity in general order and particular content of Matthew, Mark, and Luke indicated some *written* copying between them—but who copied from whom?

Next, the dominant scholarly consensus was—and is—that Matthew and Luke copied from Mark as their major common source and, therefore, as interpretations of an interpretation of an interpretation. Then, given that basis, it was also clear that another source was present since Matthew and Luke had extensive common material not found in Mark—named *Q* from *Quelle*, German for (that other) *source*, and hence, also, the letter *Q* in English.[1]

That common material indicated that *Q* was a consecutive *written* source rather than isolated oral traditions—compare, for example, the verbatim accounts of John the Baptist from *Q* in Matt 3:7–12 and Luke 3:7–9,16–17. As such, this gospel-version dates to the 50s before the devastation of Galilee in the Judeo-Roman war of 66–74 CE.

Finally, of course, *The Gospel according to Q* is not extant in any ancient manuscript. But granted Mark as source for the triple agreements between Mark, Matthew, and Luke, *Q* is a necessary hypothesis for the double agreements between Matthew and Luke, not taken from Mark.

In terms of its theology, *The Gospel according to Q* certainly accepts the Pharisaic-sectarian theology that proclaims universal resurrection for general judgment and eternal sanctions at the end of human time:

> The queen of the South will rise (*egerthēsetai*) at the judgment with the people of this generation and condemn them, because she came from the ends of the earth to listen to the wisdom of Solomon, and see, something greater than Solomon is here!
>
> The people of Nineveh will rise up (*anastēsontai*) at the judgment with this generation and condemn it, because they repented at the proclamation of Jonah, and see, something greater than Jonah is here! (*Q* in Luke 11:31–32=Matt 12:41–42)

---

[1] It is almost impossible to get a sense of *Q*'s overall content without separating it critically from Matthew and Luke. For an example, see Mark M. Mattison, "The Gospel of *Q*," Gospel.net, https://www.gospels.net/quelle.

Despite those twin texts, there is no mention of Jesus' Resurrection and no assertion that he will condemn "this generation" in the final judgment of all humanity. For *Q,* the Resurrection of Jesus is completely absent because it is theologically irrelevant.

Still, there is this other text in which Jesus laments over Jerusalem and promises or threatens return:

> Jerusalem, Jerusalem, the city that kills the prophets and stones those who are sent to it! How often have I desired to gather your children together as a hen gathers her brood under her wings, and you were not willing! See, your house is left to you. And I tell you, you will not see me until the time comes when you say, "Blessed is the one who comes in the name of the Lord." (*Q* in Luke 13:34–35=Matt 23:37–39)

At the very most, that text *may* mean that *The Gospel according to Q* implicitly presumes Jesus' ascension pending eventual return. But, in any case, it is return not ascension that gets the emphasis in that gospel-version.

I start this chapter's due diligence on sources with *Q* for two reasons. The general one is as therapy against the presumption that, from the very beginning, from Easter Sunday morning, as it were, the only way to speak of Jesus' exaltation or vindication was by Resurrection. The specific reason is as a preparation for Paul to follow in this chapter and, of course, throughout the whole book. For Paul, Resurrection (*Anastasis*) was ever and always the only way to name that exaltation.

The Gospel according to Paul

That just-seen written *Gospel according to Q* was dated to the 50s in the Jewish homeland, centered on small villages like Capernaum, Bethsaida, and Chorazin around the Galilean Lake, and worked with sayings of Jesus as divine Wisdom. The written *Gospel according to Paul* was dated to those same 50s in the Jewish diaspora, centered on great cities like Antioch, Ephesus, and Rome around the Mediterranean Sea, and worked with letters about Jesus as divine Lord.

The scholarly consensus is that there are seven original, historical, and authentic letters of Paul (Romans, 1–2 Corinthians, Galatians, Philippians, 1 Thessalonians, and Philemon)—although there may be conflations within them and insertions to them. The other six attributed to him are *probably* (Colossians, Ephesians, 2 Thessalonians) or *certainly* (1–2 Timothy, and Titus) post-, pseudo-, and often even anti-Pauline in some content. In other words, Paul was a theological minefield or, better, all mine and no field—to his credit then and his challenge still.

Apart from differences in genre between the gospel-version of *Q*, with sayings by Jesus, and that of Paul, with letters about Jesus, the most striking, surprising, and fascinating difference is that the Resurrection of Jesus is irrelevant for *Q* but dominant for Paul. He is emphatically clear and theologically emphatic on the Resurrection of Jesus—using those same two root terms as *Q* did for Queen of Sheba (*egeirō*) and the Ninevites (*anistēmi*).

At most, *The Gospel according to Q* presumed implicitly the transcultural theology of Ascension (*apotheōsis*) while *The Gospel according to Paul* proclaimed explicitly the pharisaic theology of Resurrection (*Anastasis*). For this present book, that comparison between those two earliest theologies of Jesus' exaltation was intended to focus the fullest possible attention on Paul's originality and to raise the following very fundamental questions.

First, was it Paul as a *Pharisee* who first used the concept "resurrection of the dead ones" (*anastasis nekrōn*) to interpret the exaltation of Jesus? Before that, was Jesus' exaltation understood as an Ascension—as now still present in, say, Mark 9:2–8; Luke 24:50–51; Acts 1:1–11?

Next, since Resurrection always intended an end-time universal event and never an individual in-time one, how could Paul, precisely as a *Pharisee*, ever speak of the individual Resurrection of Jesus—as distinct from his individual Ascension?

Finally, remember that, in Western Christianity, Jesus arises alone but in Eastern Christianity he arises with the whole human race personified in Adam and Eve. Which of those visions is in greater continuity with and greater conformity to Paul's understanding of Jesus' Resurrection? Put another way, would Paul be more at home with

Western or Eastern iconography of Jesus' Resurrection? Would he consider the Western tradition as Ascension (*Apotheōsis*) rather than Resurrection (*Anastasis*)?

The Gospel according to Luke-Acts

This title requires immediate justification because *The Gospel according to Luke* is the third and *The Acts of the Apostles* is the fifth book in the present New Testament order. Why combine here what is separate there? What is this *Gospel according to Luke-Acts?* Why is it of special importance alongside The *Gospel according to Paul* for this book?

First, only so many pages could be glued together to form an ancient *papyrus* scroll because too many would make the outer ones burst asunder when the scroll was fully rolled up and also make the whole too awkward to handle when it was unrolled spindle to spindle for reading. Hence, for example, Josephus needed one scroll—or volume, from volumen, Latin for scroll—for his *Life*, two for his *Against Apion,* seven for his *Jewish War,* and twenty for his *Jewish Antiquities.* The number of volumes/scrolls required for an ancient papyrus book was a constraint of container over content and medium over message.

Next, the gospel-versions of those anonymous authors traditionally named Mark, John, and Matthew with, respectively, over eleven, fifteen, and eighteen thousand words in Greek could each fit on a single scroll. But *The Gospel of Luke-Acts* required over thirty-eight thousand words and that required two scrolls with around 19,450 words in the first scroll/volume and 18,500 in the second. Luke-Acts was originally planned, completely structured, and initially produced as a single two-volume work—and the forward and backward links in Luke-Acts are as clear—or clearer—than those in *Against Apion.*

Unfortunately, however, in the canonical arrangement of the New Testament library, the two-volume book of Luke-Acts was separated by place and name to become *The Gospel according to Luke* and *The Acts of the Apostles.* The cost was the loss of authorial intention, literary purpose, rhetorical strategy, and any reader's comprehension of each volume as part of a unified whole.

Finally, then, why did Luke-Acts alone need such a single two-volume Gospel-version? What was so special and so lengthy about the thematic vision of its Good News that Luke-Acts alone required two scrolls/volumes for its proclamation?[2]

The generative vision of *The Gospel according to Luke-Acts* is that Roman Christianity and not Jewish Christianity is the future of the Messianic/Christic community; that, with Jesus, the Holy Spirit has moved from Nazareth through Samaria to Jerusalem in volume 1 and, with Paul, from Jerusalem through Samaria to Rome in volume 2; and that God's holy city is no longer Jerusalem but Rome.

Luke-Acts' generative vision employs and empowers three constitutive themes that circle around from last back to first and connect as a perfect ring of apologetical defense: First, Internal Messianic/Christic Harmony: those communities work together in communal harmony, peaceful discussion, and mini-senatorial procedure (Acts 15); Next, External Jewish Turmoil: any social disturbances come not from them but from the murderous response of Jewish "jealousy" (Luke 4:28–30; Acts 13:50; 21:30)—and sometimes also from pagan greed (Acts 16:16–19; 19:33–34); Finally, Official Roman Exculpation: every Roman official who encounters Christian leaders declares them innocent of any Roman crime. One example will suffice—for now—but it is actually intended to be a paradigmatic example for Luke-Acts and I quote it therefore in full:

> When Gallio was proconsul of Achaia, the Jews made a united attack on Paul and brought him before the tribunal. They said, "This man is persuading people to worship God in ways that are contrary to the law." Just as Paul was about to speak, Gallio said to the Jews, "If it

---

[2] My answer presumes and summarizes the sections on "The Gospel according to Luke-Acts" in John Dominic Crossan, *The Power of Parable* (San Francisco, CA: HarperOne, 2012), 197–218; and more fully in *Render unto Caesar* (San Francisco, CA: HarperOne, 2022), 105–207. From now on, I use *Luke-Acts* (with "it") for that two-volume book by an unknown author traditionally named *Luke* (with "he"); its corresponding adjective will be *Lukan;* and *Luke* or *Acts* followed by verses will designate that single book's volume I or volume 2.

were a matter of crime or serious villainy, I would be justified in accepting the complaint of you Jews; but since
it is a matter of questions about words and names and
your own law, see to it yourselves; I do not wish to be a
judge of these matters." And he dismissed them from the
tribunal. Then all of them seized Sosthenes, the official
of the synagogue, and beat him in front of the tribunal.
But Gallio paid no attention to any of these things. (Acts
18:12–17)

Lucius Junius Gallio, compelled to commit suicide with his younger brother Seneca for treasonous conspiracy against Nero in 65,
was resident in Corinth as proconsul of Achaia in 52. If the above
account were historical, it would date Paul at Corinth in that year
and the seduction of that chronological gift has rendered it almost
universally accepted within scholarship. In my best historical judgment, however, Acts 18:12–17 is a fictional manifesto deliberately
proclaimed by the most famous Roman official Paul ever encounters.

   To my mind, that account embodies in Gallio the ideal attitude Luke-Acts imagines from Roman power and thereby unites
completely together those three just-seen constitutive themes of
Internal Messianic/Christic Harmony, External Jewish Turmoil,
and Official Roman Exculpation. Unfortunately, however, a fictional
apologetic does not become a historical one by including a factual
person, a factual place, and a calculable date. Recall, always, that single word that culminates, terminates, and summarizes everything in
Luke-Acts. With Paul finally proclaiming Jesus as the Messiah/Christ
in Rome itself, that last word is *akōlytōs* or "unhindered" (Acts 28:31).
That is all Luke-Acts expects from Roman power.

   There are two major conclusions from that understanding of
The *Gospel according to Luke-Acts*. Here they are in preliminary summary but this will need to be verified again and again throughout this
book.

   One is that wherever Luke-Acts makes large-scale changes on
Mark—that is, on the major source for its first volume—we must
judge whether they are historically accurate or apologetically invented to

support Luke-Acts' generative vision. For example: it was not history but that second polemical theme of Jewish riotous jealousy through which Luke-Acts invented those murderous Jews at Nazareth. Just compare Luke's inaugural day of lethal failure at Nazareth in 4:14–30 with its source in that inaugural day of brilliant success at Capernaum in Mark 1:21–34.

Another is that wherever Luke-Acts contradicts Paul or asserts material over and above what is contained in those original Pauline letters, we must once again judge whether they are historically accurate or apologetically invented to support Luke-Acts' generative vision. For example, when Paul escaped guarded Damascus through the wall in a basket, it was not history but that same anti-Jewish theme by which Luke-Acts said polemically that it was "the Jews" seeking "to kill" him (Acts 9:23–25) but Paul said historically that it was the Nabateans seeking to arrest him (2 Cor 11:32–33).

The problem is not that Luke-Acts lacks information. He has *The Gospel according to Mark* and *The Gospel according to Q* as his major sources for Jesus. He has *The Gospel according to Paul* and certainly knows his sites—maybe even knows his epistles—as a major source for Paul. We can, therefore, watch Luke-Acts at work, respect its authorial intention, literary purpose, rhetorical strategy, and narrative tactics.

Neither is the problem that Luke-Acts lacks understanding. The second century saw many philosophical defenses of the Christian faith but Luke-Acts started that century with a narrative defense. Its purpose was what today we call controlling the narrative—and we must always wonder—then and now—how far such narrative apologetics may be from the truth, the whole truth, and nothing but the truth.

The standard pro-Roman narrative in Josephus and Tacitus was that "Christians" were the suspect followers of an executed "Christ." To that, Luke-Acts offered a counter-narrative, an *Apologia pro Vita Christiana,* a brilliantly fictionalized version that made that faith "safe" for Romans who accepted it and from Romans who attacked it (*asphaleia* in Luke 1:4 is "safety" rather than" truth," despite the NRSV translation).

Luke-Acts is the only source in the New Testament that glimpsed the future correctly and, in so doing, helped start it happening. But the price for its preview of Constantine in his fourth-century future was a prejudice against Paul in his first-century past. It is necessary in this book, therefore, to read Luke-Acts carefully and critically within its own generative vision and within that vision's three constitutive themes.

————·····:=====+=+◇+==+=====:·····————

We saw above that, already by the 50s, the two written versions, *The Gospel according to Q* and *The Gospel according to Paul* differed radically on using Resurrection to express the vindication and exaltation of Jesus—for *Q* it was absent because irrelevant, for Paul it was present because fundamental. How, now, does Jesus' Resurrection in Paul compare with *The Gospel according to Luke-Acts?* Although it regularly asserts Jesus' resurrection, does that metaphor mean the same there as in Paul? What if Luke-Acts talks of Jesus' Resurrection but understands it simply as renewed life pending final Ascension?

On the one hand, Paul identifies himself as one "circumcised on the eighth day, a member of the people of Israel, of the tribe of Benjamin, a Hebrew born of Hebrews; as to the law, a Pharisee" (Phil 3:5). Luke-Acts agrees, explicitly connects being a Pharisee with belief in "the resurrection of the dead ones" (*anastasis nekrōn*), and has Paul mocked at Athens for mentioning it before the Areopagus (Acts 17:32). Luke-Acts certainly knows Pharisaic claims about "the resurrection of the dead ones" (Acts 23:6,8).

In the first volume of Luke-Acts, however, that term is limited to "the resurrection of the righteous" (Luke 14:14). Also, while copying Mark 12:18–27 about the resurrected wife with seven resurrected husbands as a gotcha-question from the "Sadducees . . . who say there is no resurrection," Luke-Acts mentions only "those who are considered worthy of a place in that age and in the resurrection from the dead" (Luke 20:35) and calls them "sons [=heirs] of God, being sons [=heirs] of the resurrection" (Luke 20:36). Still, in its second volume, Luke-Acts has Paul speak of "a resurrection of both the righteous and the unrighteous" (Acts 24:15). For Luke-Acts, is "the resurrection of the dead" universal for all or particular for some?

Be that as it may, Jesus' Resurrection is certainly connected to the "resurrection of the dead" in Luke-Acts. The Sadducees—once again—were annoyed because Peter and John were "proclaiming in Jesus the resurrection of the dead" (Acts 4:2, note literal translation). Furthermore, Jesus is even described as "the first from the resurrection of the dead"—*prōtos ex anastaseōs nekrōn* (Acts 26:23, note literal translation). That is very close to the historical Paul's own formulation that "Christ has been raised from the dead, the first fruits of those who have died" (1 Cor 15:20, literally "have slept").

On the other hand, despite such mentions of Jesus' Resurrection there are several indications that, for Luke-Acts, the meaning of Resurrection is simply Ascension.

First, watch how Luke-Acts adopts but adapts two narratives about Jesus' Resurrection from its source in Mark. About mid-way through Mark's gospel-version, a story tells how, "on a high mountain apart, by themselves," Peter, James, and John saw Jesus "transfigured before them":

> His clothes became dazzling white, such as no one on earth could bleach them. And there appeared to them Elijah with Moses, who were talking with Jesus . . . Then a cloud overshadowed them, and from the cloud there came a voice, "This is my Son, the Beloved; listen to him!" (Mark 9:2–4,7).

Before Mark, that was originally an ascension transfiguration with the message of the departing Jesus certified and mandated by God. The most striking proof is the presence of two major Jewish figures who had already ascended into heaven. Elijah had been assumed there by a chariot of fire in a whirlwind (2 Kings 2:11). Moses, as we saw in Chapter 1, had also ascended to heaven, not however from the positive vision of an eyewitness but from the negative witness of an unknown grave. But, in Mark's usage, after that vision of ascension is over, the text concludes with this injunction from Jesus:

> As they were coming down the mountain, Jesus ordered them to tell no one about what they had seen, until after the Son of Man had risen from the dead *(ek nekrōn anastēi)*.

So they kept the matter to themselves, questioning what
this rising from the dead (*ek nekrōn anastēnai*) could mean.
(9:9–10)

At the top of the mountain in pre-Markan tradition, the vision was
of Jesus' Ascension but, at the bottom of the mountain in Markan
redaction, the promise was of Jesus' Resurrection.

Luke-Acts takes that account from its Markan source but makes
significant changes on it. Moses and Elijah are there, of course, but,
"they appeared in glory and were speaking of his departure (*exodon*),
which he was about to accomplish at Jerusalem" (Luke 9:31). Following that insertion, Luke-Acts omits the Markan admonition about
silence pending "resurrection" and says only that, "they kept silent
and in those days told no one any of the things they had seen" (Luke
9:36b). Luke-Acts takes the Transfiguration as an ascension that is
prophetic of its other two ascensions in Luke 24:50–52 and Acts
1:2,9–11.

Next, here is another major change about Resurrection by
Luke-Acts on its Markan source. Mark's story of the empty tomb
would immediately indicate either grave-robbery or ascension to the
standard first-century hearer.[3] Mark quickly corrects any such misap-
prehension: "You are looking for Jesus of Nazareth, who was crucified. He has been raised" (16:6). Luke-Acts rephrases Mark with this:
"Why do you look for the living among the dead? He is not here, but
has risen" (Luke 24:5b). Before you read "risen" Luke-Acts prepares
you to understand it as "living" once again.

Luke-Acts also adds to the Emmaus story that when the wom-
en "did not find his body there, they came back and told us that they

---

[3] In the first century CE, Chariton of Aphrodisias' novel *Callirhoe* 3.3-5 had
that murdered woman's husband, Chaereas, visit her tomb "at dawn," discover "the
stones removed," and "decide to go in." Onlookers suggested "tomb robbers" but
Chaereas presumed that she had been assumed by some God or that he had "a
Goddess as my wife and did not know it, and she was above our human lot." See
Chariton, *Callirhoe*. Loeb's Classical Library. Translated by G. P. Goold (Cambridge,
MA: Harvard University Press, 1995), pages 144-147.

had indeed seen a vision of angels who said that he was alive" (Luke 24:23). Following on that interpretation of Resurrection as coming-alive-again, when Jesus asks for food, "they gave him a piece of broiled fish, and he took it and ate in their presence" (Luke 24:41b–43).

Finally, with Resurrection interpreted as coming back to life again with a rather ordinary body capable of eating, the way is open for Luke-Acts to hinge its twin volumes with two different—and traditional?—accounts of Ascension: "he withdrew from them and was carried up into heaven" (Luke 24:51) and "he was taken up to heaven . . . as they were watching, he was lifted up, and a cloud took him out of their sight" (Acts 1:2,9). Notice that connection between that divine "cloud" in Acts 2:9 and the earlier one mentioned twice in Luke's revision of Mark's Transfiguration story (Luke 9:34). And recall that transcultural ascension "cloud" seen earlier for Moses in Josephus (*JA* 4.326) and Romulus in Livy's *History of Rome* (1:16).

In summary. Paul and Luke-Acts agree in speaking of Jesus' Resurrection with the same noun *anastasis* and the same verb *egeirō* and agree in connecting Jesus' Resurrection to the "resurrection of the dead" with the same phrase, *anastasis nekrōn*. But, as we shall see again and again in this book, the problem with Luke-Acts is not with its Pauline information but with its non-Pauline or even anti-Pauline interpretation, not with Pauline content but with non-Pauline or anti-Pauline meaning. Paul says "resurrection" and intends resurrection as understood within Jewish-Pharisaic tradition; Luke-Acts says "resurrection" but intends ascension as understood within—of course—Roman transcultural tradition.

--- ·······✦······· ---

Whether you understand Ascension and Resurrection literally or metaphorically (I do the latter) what is at stake in those concepts for non-biblical, non-religious, non-theistic people? Ascension imagines, accepts, and thereby creates a world in which extraordinary individuals are accorded immortal Super Hero (but seldom Super Heroine) status. We may no longer imagine such persons as having ascended to divinity but we still celebrate and commemorate them as having ascended to super-humanity—despite, to repeat, the salvific narcosis of Super Heroes who never die and the toxic danger of Super Leaders who never lose.

What then about Resurrection? It is a metaphor of eventual and final cosmic justice with the following scenario—as cited by Paul. First, the dead would arise alongside those then living: "in a moment, in the twinkling of an eye, at the last trumpet. For the trumpet will sound, and the dead will be raised imperishable, and we will be changed" (1 Cor 15:52). Next, "we will all stand before the judgment seat of God" (Rom 14:10). Finally, from that judgment will come rewards or punishments: "all of us must appear before the judgment seat of Christ, so that each may receive recompense for what has been done in the body, whether good or evil" (2 Cor 5:10).

In those last two quotations, the change from "the judgment seat of God" to "the judgment seat of Christ" indicates Paul's vocation-revelation but that is the subject for the next chapter. To end this chapter, I focus on the purely Judeo-Pharisaic vision of the resurrection of the dead before the judgment seat of God apart from any later Pauline messianization of that expectation.

That Pharisaic claim was of universal bodily resurrection, universal bodily judgment, and universal bodily "recompense"—be it for "good" (in heaven) or for "evil" (in hell). Taken literally, I consider that to be transcendental terrorism laced with ludicrous and preposterous elements. Taken metaphorically, as it should be, I find in it a searing challenge for our species.

Recall, from the conclusion in Chapter 1, the escalatory violence of our species against the physical environment, other species, and ourselves. If that triple onslaught continues its acceleration, the question is whether our species is ultimately sustainable. The answer to that question will not be determined by some inevitable end-time moment but by how every single member of our species has acted, now acts, and will act to continue or discontinue our escalatory destruction of the physical, feral, and human worlds. If we continue it and some final day arrives, the whole human race will arise before the judgment seat not of divine punishments but of human consequences. Finally, we might wonder how a two-thousand-year-old sectarian Jewish theology caught the approaching shadow of our present evolutionary crisis.

Chapter 3

"AS TO THE LAW, A PHARISEE"

He understands himself to be an apostle of the Jews to the
Gentiles and understands this as a calling. In Galatians there
is nothing about a conversion in the sense of being over-
whelmed. Rather there is a calling . . . an apostle *from the Jews*
to the nations.

—Jacob Taubes, *The Political Theology of Paul.*

Think about two books from the start of the last century that described Paul's "conversion," an event which this present book prefers to call Paul's "vocation-revelation." Both started as prestigious
lecture series by Harvard professors, both focused on individual
psychological experience over communal sociological tradition, and
both became classics not despite but because of that focus.

In the second of his two lectures on "Conversion" William
James[1] had to

> finish the subject of Conversion, considering at first those
> striking instantaneous instances of which Saint Paul's is
> the most eminent, and in which, often amid tremendous
> emotional excitement or perturbation of the senses, a
> complete division is established in the twinkling of an eye
> between the old life and the new. (Lecture X, page 217)

Notice three elements in that understanding of "conversion" in general and of Paul's experience in particular: it is instantaneous, in the

---

[1] William James, *The Varieties of Religious Experience: A Study in Human Nature.*
The Gifford Lectures at Edinburgh in 1901-1902. New York: Longmans, Green,
& Co., 1912. Read online from *Project Gutenberg.*

twinkling of an eye; it involves emotional and even physical disturbances; it establishes a complete division between old and new life.

I admit immediately that I do not think a "conversion" is ever
"instantaneous, in the twinkling of an eye." Even if externally it appears as a sudden personal transformation, it must have had internally
some progressive period of change and some fundamental abiding
continuity lest a "conversion" experience constitute a psychotic break
from reality. That, at least, is my own understanding of our common
humanity.

Next, Arthur Darby Nock[2]—who once praised James' as the
only book about religion worth taking with you to a desert island—
wrote that, for Paul,

> to become a Christian meant in the first instance a com-
> plete change of face. It is the first conversion to Christi-
> anity of which we have knowledge. He brought to it not
> merely a fresh enthusiasm but also an imperious inner
> need to discover an interpretation and reconciliation of
> the old and the new in his religious life. (page 191)

That description echoes only the last two of James' three criteria:
James' "complete division" between the old and new life reappears
as Nock's "complete change" between the old and new religious life.
Also, James' "emotional excitement" connects with Nock's "imperious inner need." But there is nothing in Nock similar to James'
description of "conversion" as "instantaneous" transition "in the
twinkling of an eye." And, as just seen, I consider that omission to
be correct.

Furthermore, James' "tremendous emotional excitement or
perturbation of the senses" and Nock's "imperious inner need to
discover an interpretation and reconciliation of the old and the new"
understands Paul's "conversion" as a psychologically driven, emo-
tionally imperative, or guiltily inevitable experience that comes from

---

[2] Arthur Darby Nock, *Conversion: The Old and the New in Religion from Alexander the Great to Augustine of Hippo.* Oxford, UK: Oxford University Press, 1933. Read
online from the Internet Archive.

a misreading of "Wretched man that I am! Who will rescue me from this body of death?" (Rom 7:24). But that *cri-de-coeur* on law and sin does not speak historically for Israel in general nor autobiographically for Paul in particular but rhetorically for all humanity represented in plaintive first-person language.

Finally, for James and Nock, for Christian interpretation and proverbial expression, it is Luke's threefold dramatization of Paul's "conversion" that determines our recollection of Paul's experience "on the road to Damascus" (Acts 9:3a; 22:6a; 26:12–13a). Hence, the present chapter tackles the following problems.

How are we to escape Luke's perfect localization of a "conversion" as happening "on the road" since the geographical transition from external place to external place mirrors and models the transformational transition from internal state to internal state?

How are we to escape Luke's perfect dramatization for a "conversion" whose protagonist is blinded by light, felled to the ground, and hears an imperious voice rather than sees a gracious sight (Acts 9:3b–4; 22:6b-7; 26:13–14)?

Yet as hard as those "how"'s may be for our memory and imagination, bracketing Luke's three biographical versions is precisely what we must do as we begin this chapter, which focuses exclusively on Paul's single autobiographical account of his "conversion." There will be time enough to consider Luke's versions in the next chapter but, for here and now, we ignore the external theatrics of Luke's versions to focus on the internal dynamics of Paul's. How, from empowering enlightenment inside rather than from blinding endarkenment outside, did Paul undergo that most famous "conversion"? We move carefully, then, and step by step—with five successive steps.

Paul the Faithful Jew

Paul's "conversion" was from what to what? Despite Nock, Paul would never have recognized himself as "the first conversion to Christianity," that is, as converting from Judaism to Christianity. Because, first and above all else, those communities did not yet exist as separate options in that early first century! Second, because the following three quotations indicate very clearly Paul's ongoing pride in, loyalty to, and acceptance of his ethnic identity:

> Are they Hebrews? So am I. Are they Israelites? So am I. Are they descendants of Abraham? So am I. (2 Cor 11:22)
>
> I could wish that I myself were accursed and cut off from Christ for the sake of my own people, my kindred according to the flesh. They are Israelites, and to them belong the adoption, the glory, the covenants, the giving of the law, the worship, and the promises; to them belong the patriarchs, and from them, according to the flesh, comes the Messiah, who is over all, God blessed forever. Amen. (Rom 9:3–5)
>
> I myself am an Israelite, a descendant of Abraham, a member of the tribe of Benjamin. (Rom 11:1)

Also, when Paul lists his ongoing dangers, he identifies some from "my own people" (2 Cor 11:26).

Luke-Acts also has Paul announce his Jewish identity twice and each time it adds on résumé upgrades about Tarsus citizenship and Gamaliel education: "I am a Jew, from Tarsus in Cilicia, a citizen of an important city" (Acts 21:39); and "I am a Jew, born in Tarsus in Cilicia, but brought up in this city [Jerusalem] at the feet of Gamaliel, educated strictly according to our ancestral law, being zealous for God" (22:3).

In none of those quotations is it possible to glimpse even a hint of "tremendous emotional excitement or perturbation of the senses" or any "imperious inner need" to convert from his accepted Abrahamic, Hebraic, or Israelite identity. In Paul's self-consciousness, his transition was not a "conversion" to Christ outside Judaism but a vocation from Christ inside Judaism.

Paul the Fervent Pharisee

Paul went far beyond simple loyalty to his native Judaism. He was ultraloyal to it and ultratraditional within it:

> I advanced in Judaism beyond many among my people
> of the same age, for I was far more zealous for the tradi-
> tions of my ancestors. (Gal 1:13–14)
>
> If anyone else has reason to be confident in the flesh,
> I have more: circumcised on the eighth day, a member of
> the people of Israel, of the tribe of Benjamin, a Hebrew
> born of Hebrews; as to the law, a Pharisee . . . as to
> righteousness under the law, blameless. (Phil 3:5–6)

No sign there of a tortured soul crying out *personally* in frustrated
impotence with law and sin as in that just-seen misreading of Rom
7:13–24. Instead, Paul asserts proudly that he was "as to the law, a
Pharisee." But what exactly was a Pharisee in that first-century Jewish
context?

Josephus cites three major "philosophical schools" in Judaism
(*JW* 2.119–166; *JA* 13:171–173; 18:11–22). But that rather innocuous
description is adopted for Greek taste and adapted to Roman control. Those were actually religio-political factions struggling for leadership against overweening Greek culture and overwhelming Roman
power in the first-century Jewish homeland. The Sadducees were the
conservative right, the Essenes the radical left, and the Pharisees the
liberal—and popular—center.

Libelous invective by Messianic/Christic Jews against Pharisaic
Jews in the gospel-stories bespeaks a bitter—because intra-familial—
struggle for that popular center. Such *ad hominem* diatribes were/are
the typical strategy of character assassination to avoid religio-political
discussion and the standard tactics of calling names to avoid debating
ideas. That febrile animosity explains, for example, the sixfold "Woe
to you, scribes and Pharisees, hypocrites" that Matt 23:13–29 retroj-
ects—unfortunately and inaccurately—onto the lips of Jesus. Bracketing such polemical invective, what exactly was a Pharisee?

All such intragospel invective aside, here is how Josephus described the core of Pharisaic theology with, as usual, its Jewish
elements pruned back for Greek taste:

> The Pharisees . . . are considered the most accurate inter-
> preters of the law, and hold the position of the leading sect.

> ... Every soul, they maintain, is imperishable, but the soul
> of the good alone passes into another body, while the souls
> of the wicked suffer eternal punishment. (*JW* 2.162-164)
>
> The Pharisees ... believe that souls have power to sur-
> vive death and that there are rewards and punishments un-
> der the earth for those who have led lives of virtue or vice:
> eternal imprisonment is the lot of evil souls; while the
> good souls receive an easy passge to a new life. (*JA* 18.14)

In that first citation, "another body" does not intend metempsy-
chosis, the transmission of souls from one body to another here on
earth, but simply that the virtuous dead receive a body in recognizable material continuity with their former self.

A footnote. Without a body of whatever material composition,
how could Aeneas, for example, have recognized the dead Trojan
hero Hector in that mutilated apparition that came to him "black
with gory dust," or recognized his dead father, Anchises, among the
dead in Hades when "thrice there he strove to throw his arms about
his neck; thrice the form, vainly clasped, fled from his hands, even
as light winds, and most like a winged dream" (Virgil, *Aeneid* 2.271;
6.700). You could and can certainly ask even respectfully about the
universal resurrection: "With what kind of body do they come?" (1
Cor 15:37) but, in dream, vision, or apparition, some kind of bodily
continuity is needed for individual recognition—be it understood as
mentally internal or physically external.

In any case, what Josephus emphasizes for the Pharisees is
both legal accuracy here and cosmic justice hereafter. That version of
cosmic justice is, as expected, adapted by a platonizing veneer—recall
Phaedo 113–14—to Greek taste with disembodied souls rather than
to Jewish taste with embodied ones. There is, of course, an obvious
contradiction for the Pharisees between fidelity to ancient tradition
and the recent invention of resurrection. They solved that contradiction by claiming an oral tradition from Mount Sinai as old as that
other written one!

That claim for eventual cosmic justice is probably what made
the Pharisees "hold the position of the leading sect" especially with
ordinary people who suffered daily from its absence. Also, remember

that the term resurrection is always shorthand for that entire vision of ultimate cosmic justice involving a tripartite sequence of universal resurrection, general judgment, and eternal sanctions—at end-time.

Once again, Luke-Acts agrees that Paul was not only a loyal Jew but a fervent Pharisee. He has Paul assert that, "I am a Pharisee, a son of Pharisees" (Acts 23:6), and that "I have belonged to the strictest sect of our religion and lived as a Pharisee" (26:5). As usual with Luke-Acts, "son of a Pharisee" upgrades Paul's résumé.

Furthermore, Luke-Acts agrees with Josephus' emphasis on Resurrection theology as the core of Pharisaic tradition and puts it in defensive speeches by Paul:

> When Paul noticed that some were Sadducees and others were Pharisees, he called out in the council, "Brothers, I am a Pharisee, a son of Pharisees. I am on trial concerning the hope of the resurrection of the dead (*anastasis nekrōn*)." When he said this, a dissension began between the Pharisees and the Sadducees, and the assembly was divided. (The Sadducees say that there is no resurrection, or angel, or spirit; but the Pharisees acknowledge all three.) (Acts 23:6–8)
>
> This one sentence that I called out while standing before them, "It is about the resurrection of the dead (*anastasis nekrōn*) that I am on trial before you today." (24:21)
>
> I have belonged to the strictest sect of our religion and lived as a Pharisee. . . . Why is it thought incredible by any of you that God raises the dead (*nekrous egeirei*)? (26:5b,8)

I cite those speeches only as correct information about Pharisees versus Sadducees on the resurrection of the dead ones and not as speeches given historically by Paul. The author of Luke-Acts is well trained in Greek rhetorical strategies for inventing speech-in-context and in literary devices for creating speech-in-character—and does it powerfully, persuasively, and persistently.

Paul the Zealous Persecutor

Here, for a third time, Paul and Luke-Acts are in agreement. Paul says that: "I was violently persecuting the church of God and was trying to destroy it" (Gal 1:13); that I was, "as to zeal, a persecutor of the church" (Phil 3:6); and that "I persecuted the church of God" (1 Cor 15:9). Luke-Acts agrees, again on Paul's own lips: "Being zealous for God . . . I persecuted this Way up to the point of death by binding both men and women and putting them in prison" (Acts 22:4–5).

First, what about the *how* of that persecution from Paul's term "zeal" and Luke's term "zealous"? The model of "zeal" in the biblical tradition is Phineas who murdered an Israelite for ethnico-legal disloyalty in marrying a Midianite woman (Num 25:6–8). In the first century, Philo claimed that, "zeal" allowed *any* person outraged religiously "to exact the penalties offhand and with no delay without bringing the offender before jury or council or any kind of magistrate at all" (*The Special Laws* 1.55). Nevertheless, in the political realities of a Roman world rather than the religious dreams of a Jewish one, Paul's destructive violence did not involve murder in Damascus. At most, he was a conservative fundamentalist and a reactionary traditionalist who, as a probably self-appointed loyalty enforcer, ejected Messianic/Christic members from his synagogue at Damascus and thereby destroyed them as falling between socio-economic and religio-political worlds.

Next, what about the *why* of that persecution. What—even minimally—must Paul have known about that "church" to make him a persecutor against it? The answer necessitates going back and starting with John the Baptist and Jesus of Nazareth. They were distinguished accurately by their enemies saying that John fasted but Jesus feasted. But one fasts in preparation for what is coming; one feasts in celebration for what is present. So: John fasted in appropriate preparation for God's Rule on earth as coming-soon but Jesus feasted in appropriate celebration for God's rule on earth as already here (*Q* in Matt 11:18–19=Luke 7:33–34).

But how could Jesus make such a stunning claim about the presence of *God's Rule* in a homeland increasingly under *Rome's Rule?*

How could such a claim be anything more than a cruel joke in a world completely unchanged under Tiberius, Pilate, and Antipas, within the ongoing Rule of Rome?

Jesus' vision was a paradigm shift, tradition swerve, or disruptive innovation within general Jewish expectation for the advent of God's Rule and/or the Messianic/Christic Age on earth—be it the prophetic one of a sometime-coming or the apocalyptic one of a soon-coming. That vision, however, involved another and concomitant change: God's Rule and/or the Messianic/Christic Age had not come as an end-time divine intervention but as an in-time divine-human collaboration. It was here on earth only by, with, in, and through human participation in its presence.

That was most clearly indicated and fully summed up in the Parable of the Mustard Seed—the only parable of Jesus with two certain versions within the New Testament itself (*Q* in Matt 13:31–32=Luke 13:18–19; and Mark in 4:30–32). Instead of God's Rule as a wild mustard seed producing a plant solely by divine action, Jesus likened it in both versions to a domestic mustard seed sown by human hand but grown—like all produce—by divine guidance. As domestic and not wild, that seed was, for *Q,* "a mustard seed that someone took and sowed in his field" (Matt 13:31) or "a mustard seed that someone took and tossed into his own garden" (Luke 13:19); and, for Mark, "a mustard seed, which, when sown upon the ground . . . when sown . . ." (4:31–32).

In summary. Paul's persecuted synagogue fellows must have proclaimed Jesus as God's awaited Messiah/Christ for whom God's Rule on earth meant that everything promised, prophesied, expected, or awaited in the Messianic/Christic Age shifted inexorably from an end-time product of divine intervention to an in-time process of divine-human collaboration.

Finally, Jesus emphasized even more clearly the divine/human collaboration in the advent of God's Rule on earth with another agricultural metaphor: "The harvest is plentiful, but the laborers are few; therefore ask the Lord of the harvest to send out laborers into his harvest" (*Q* in Matt 9:37–38=Luke 10:2). Put bluntly: it's a covenant, dummy! For what is a more biblical term than "covenant" but that term presumes a two-way operation, a participation, a collaboration between two protagonists—even if one is divine and the other human.

Paul the Apostolic Convert

It is clear from Paul's letter that the Galatians were disputing his authority by claiming he was but a subordinate delegate from the apostles in Jerusalem and was not even their faithful representative but simply "seeking human approval" and "trying to please people" (Gal 1:10). In stern rebuttal, Paul insists that during his vocation-revelation, "I did not confer with any human being nor did I go up to Jerusalem to those who were already apostles before me. . . . Then after three years I did go up to Jerusalem . . . [for] fifteen days" (1:16b–18). Paul was called directly by God and not sub-called by the Jerusalem apostles.

In that polemical context Paul describes his vocation as a divinely controlled rather than a humanly planned change from persecutor to proclaimer:

> You have heard, no doubt, of my earlier life in Judaism. I was violently persecuting the church of God and was trying to destroy it . . . . God, who had set me apart before I was born and called me through his grace, was pleased to reveal his Son to me, so that I might proclaim him among the Gentiles. (1:13–16)

Still, within the external polemics about his vocation in the letter to the Galatians, Paul gives us no information about its internal dynamics within his own heart, mind, and conscience. But there is, however, one very definite if also very delicate hint. Watch how Paul describes his divine calling with echoes from the equally divine vocations of the two greatest prophets in biblical tradition. Here are those three divine calls:

> *Isaiah* in 49:1: "Listen to me, O coastlands, pay attention, you nations *(ethnē)* from far away! The Lord called

me before I was born, while I was in my mother's womb he named me."

Jeremiah in 1:5: "Before I formed you in the womb I knew you, and before you were born I consecrated you; I appointed you a prophet to the nations (*ethnē*)."

Paul in Gal 1:15–16a: "God, who had set apart (*aphorisas*) me before I was born and called me through his grace, was pleased to reveal (*apokalypsai*) his Son to me, so that I might proclaim him among the Gentiles (*ethnē*)."

First, both Isaiah and Jeremiah are cited in special relationship with the nations or the Gentiles (*ethnē*). Such, then, was also Paul's vocation—to the nations or Gentiles (*ethnē*). Second, however, both Isaiah and Jeremiah use poetic parallelism to assert the primordial nature of their call, as does Paul but with a significant difference:

Isaiah:	"before I was born while I was in my mother's womb."
Jeremiah:	"in the womb before you were born."
Paul:	"before I was born, God, who had set apart (*aphorisas*) me."

That last phrase must have been important for Paul because he repeated it in that most formal of all his letter openings: "Paul, a servant of Jesus Christ, called to be an apostle, set apart (*aphōrismenos*) for the gospel of God" (Rom 1:1).[3]

The term *Pharisaios* in Greek just like *Pharisee* in English derives from the Hebrew and Aramaic words for *one-set-apart* or *one-separated-out* from others and even if that name was a jibe from those others, it could be boast for the one in question. But does Paul cite his identity of "Pharisee" positively as he does that of "Jew" or negatively as he

---

[3] Giorgio Agamben, *The Time that Remains: A Commentary on the Letter to the Romans.* Trans. Patricia Dailey (Stanford: Stanford University Press, 2005) writes that, in using "'separated,' Paul thus alludes, in an ironic, albeit cruelly ironic fashion to his separation of times past, his segregation as a Pharisee" (page 46).

does that of "persecutor"? Is his original Pharisaic identity part of his abandoned past or his permanent present?

For myself, Paul was, is, and should always be seen as a *Pharisaic Jew* because that is what gave him that theology of end-time resurrection/judgment/sanction that he applied to Jesus as the in-time Messiah/Christ. Paul's Pharisaic faith remained an ever-consistent facet of his self-conscious identity and, furthermore, was the ground on which he pivoted from an anti-Messianic/Christic Pharisee to a pro-Messianic/Christic Pharisee.

Here is how I see the inner dynamics of Paul's vocation-revelation. He first persecuted those who said that, with Jesus and his community, the Messianic/Christic Age of God's Rule on earth was already present here below. But, if so, his Pharisaic faith in end-time resurrection/judgment, and eternal sanctions was wrong—or if right, where were those events present in the world now? Then came the epiphanic revelation: what if those events were already here too but as in-time process rather than end-time product—as those he had persecuted claimed for the Messianic/Christic Age of God's Rule? Still, how was that possible and credible: how could the end-time universal resurrection, general judgment, and eternal sanctions be an in-time process rather than an end-time product? Watch how, later, he defended that inaugural intuition—in two texts, the second of which is as small and explosive as an atom.

Paul the Messianic/Christic Pharisee

Think, as prologue, about some counter-facts. What if Jesus' life had been exactly as we know it from the gospel-versions, but he had never been executed? What if he had been widely accepted as the Messiah/Christ but had never died on a Roman cross? What if he had lived a long life teaching, healing, and parabling God's Rule and died peacefully at home in Nazareth? Or conversely, what if Jesus had been rejected but with scorn and mockery rather than with flogging and crucifying? Would Paul, could Paul, have ever been converted to become a Messianic/Christic Pharisee if Jesus had not died as the "Messiah/Christ crucified" (1 Cor 1:23; 2:2)?

Whatever is understood about Ascension, Paul could never have imagined Resurrection without Crucifixion. That was always and ever God's Resurrection of God's Crucified Messiah/Christ. It was the injustice of executing God's Messiah/Christ that started God's justification of the world here and now in time. That is why 1 Corinthians opens on the Crucifixion and closes on the Resurrection. For Paul, Crucifixion and Resurrection are two sides of the same coin—and you cannot have a one-sided coin. What, then, about Resurrection?

A First Text (1 Cor 15:12–20). Some members of the Corinthian community—probably with the most platonic presuppositions—denied the possibility of any universal *bodily* resurrection: "some of you say there is no resurrection of the dead" (*anastasis nekrōn*) and "someone will ask, 'How are the dead raised? With what kind of body do they come?'" (15:12b,35). In rebuttal Paul insists:

> *If* Christ is proclaimed as raised from the dead
> (*ek nekrōn egēgertai*)
>> how can some of you say there is no resurrection
>> of the dead (*anastasis nekrōn*)?
> *If* there is no resurrection of the dead (*anastasis nekrōn*),
>> then Christ has not been raised (*egēgertai*) . . .
> *If* the dead are not raised (*nekroi ouk egeirontai*)
>> then Christ has not been raised (*egēgertai*).
> *But in fact* Christ has been raised from the dead
> (*egēgertai ek nekrōn*),
>> the first fruits of those who have died. (15:12,13,16,20)

In those three *Ifs*, Paul argues first from Christ's resurrection to the universal resurrection and then twice from the universal resurrection to Christ's.

In other words, the resurrection of Jesus and the resurrection of the dead ones stand or fall together because "resurrection" meant a universal end-time event before it ever could have meant an individual in-time case. Also, it could only mean an individual case if included in the universal one. Resurrection—unlike Ascension—was never an individual but always a universal operation. How then did

Paul-the-*Pharisee* understand that reciprocity of individual case and universal destiny? Watch the metaphor he uses, in 15:20:

> Christ has been raised from the dead (*egēgertai ek nekrōn*)
> the first fruits of those who have slept (*kekoimēmenōn*)

To repeat: the resurrection of Jesus stands or falls with the resurrection of the dead ones—and so the verb *egeiro* is used alike for both. Paul's chosen metaphor for the universal resurrection is the harvest of earth and Jesus is "the first fruits" (15:20,23). But, first fruits and full harvest come or go together. You could not have one without the other and harvest is an ongoing in-time process from start to finish. In biblical law, for example, God had to receive "the first fruits of your grain, your wine, and your oil, as well as the first of the fleece of your sheep" (Deut 18:4). But "first fruits" was, in effect, the first ritual act of a harvest which thereafter continued as an ongoing process to its completion.

That metaphor for resurrection did not entail two disjointed termini of start and finish with no ongoing process between them. As, for Jesus, *God's Rule* was now a collaborative in-time process rather than an interventionist end-time product, so, for Paul, *God's Resurrection* was also a collaborative in-time process rather than an interventionist end-time product.

A Second Text (Rom 1:4). The incantatory hymnic opening of what turned out to be Paul's last letter is carefully formulated as a striking balance in the Greek text:

> Paul, servant of *Jesus Christ, called to be an apostle,* set apart
> for the gospel of God, which he promised beforehand
> through his prophets in the holy scriptures,
>> the gospel concerning *his Son,*
>>> by the seed of David (*ek spermatos David*)
>>> *according to* the flesh
>> was declared to be *Son of God* with power
>>> *according to* the spirit of holiness
>>> by resurrection of dead ones (*ex anastaseōs nekrōn*)
> *Jesus Christ* our Lord, through whom we have received

grace and *apostleship* to bring about the obedience of faith among all the Gentiles for the sake of his name, including yourselves who are *called* to belong to Jesus Christ. (Rom 1:1–6)

The outermost frames match these three main words: *Jesus Christ, called, apostleship*. The next inner frames balance Jesus the Christ as God's Son both in the flesh and in the spirit. The innermost balance is the core of this hymnic rhapsody. Focus for now on that terminal phrase, which, all too often, is translated as "by his resurrection from the dead" as in the older Revised Standard Version. That was later corrected into "by resurrection from the dead" in the New Revised Standard Version. Still, no matter how translated, most readers understand that phrase to mean: "by Jesus' resurrection from the dead."

That misunderstands Paul rather completely because Rom 1:4 must be read as a succinct summary of that just-seen 1 Cor 15:12–20: the resurrection of Jesus and the resurrection of the dead ones stand or fall together. In fact, the former is subsumed into and inside the latter. The Messianic/Christic resurrection of Jesus is the "first fruits" of the Pharisaic resurrection of all humanity. Paul is a *Pharisaic* Messianic/Christic or, maybe more accurately, a Messianic/Christic *Pharisee*. Listen carefully to Rom 1:4 because that sound you hear in the background is the heartbeat of Paul.

One footnote. In Rom 1:1–4, note that combination of "the resurrection of the dead ones" and "among all the Gentiles." Within the inner dynamics of his vocation-revelation, it was his Pharisaic faith in the absolute universality of "the resurrection of the dead ones" that led necessarily to his Messianic/Christic vocation as apostle "among all the Gentiles." It was, therefore, "the resurrection of the dead ones" as in-time process that established and specified the foundation of universalism for Paul.

Those majestic texts—in full as 1 Cor 15:12–58 and Rom 1:1–6 —represent the core of Paul's empowering vision but it raises these questions—then and now. What did it mean that the universal resurrection, the general judgment, and eternal sanctions in heaven and hell were already started? What did it mean that Messianic/Christics were called to live resurrected lives and thereby create heaven rather than hell as an ongoing process on this earth? What did it mean that the execution of Jesus the Messiah/Christ was an act of cosmic injustice that brought *cosmic justice* into time as an ongoing process rather than leaving it out of time as an end-time product?

—·····⋯⋯⋯═════★◇★═════⋯⋯⋯·····—

Before I turn to the next chapter, I pause to consider whether and how it is possible to hear Paul's message from pre-enlightenment antiquity into contemporary post-enlightenment modernity—if that is where you and I are now. That question of contemporary relevance is justified and even demanded because Paul—like Jesus before him—claimed a vision not just for his own time and place but for all times and all places. He should, therefore, be judged for either overweening impertinence or overwhelming relevance.

First, for Paul, within his Jewish and biblical tradition, God is the Supreme Being who existed before the universe, created it, and will continue without or after it. This God of distributive justice sanctioned the world with rewards and punishments—the latter mitigated totally by forgiveness or partially by mercy. Paul's theory of cosmic justice as in-time process rather than end-time product is grounded on the existence of that biblical God. If that God is not credible for you, me, us, is the cosmic justice of that God equally irrelevant?

Second, we can argue *ad infinitum* and possibly *ad nauseam* about theism versus atheism, monotheism versus polytheism, this God versus that God. But, the universe, with or without the *Big God of Creation,* still has and always had the *Big Bang of Creation.* Evolution was, is, and will be there whether we are theists or atheists, was always there before we knew about it, and is still there whether we accept it or not. Therefore, my strategy in this book is not to deny or debate God but, bracketing God, to focus on human evolution within cosmic evolution and to see how Paul's message looks through that lens.

Third, through that lens of evolution, divine punishments reappear as human consequences; divine forgiveness reappears as our human capacity for change; and divine mercy reappears as the human time available for change before it is too late forever. Paul's message of universal resurrection, general judgment, and eternal recompense as an in-time process is a prescient indictment of what we have done and are doing. The universal resurrection, the rising up of every single person who has lived or will ever live leads to a general judgment of how each and every one of us has operated on earth to create our own eternal recompense of heaven or hell here below. Paul's cosmic justice is relevant as a metaphor of human responsibility, as a parable of human accountability, and as a powerfully persuasive cost-accounting for our violence as *Homo sapiens* on one another, on other species, and on our environment.

Chapter 4

"I SAW A LIGHT FROM HEAVEN, BRIGHTER THAN THE SUN"

Whenever Paul addresses his writings, he always draws attention to the fact that he has been entitled to speak . . . suddenly, on the road to Damascus (if, as we believe, in this particular instance one can, for once and once only, trust this fabricated biography of Paul that the New Testament presents under the title Acts of the Apostles).

—Alain Badiou, *Saint Paul: The Foundation of Universalism*

Actually, the account—or three accounts—of Paul's vocation "on the road to Damascus" is a "particular instance" where we must absolutely not trust the "fabricated biography of Paul" in the New Testament's Acts of the Apostles. The problem is not Luke's dramatic theatricals in the noon-day sun—those are protected by poetic license. The problem is that, for his divine vocation, the Lukan-Paul deviates most seriously and deliberately from the Pauline-Paul by quietly questioning and subtly subverting his identity, authority, and integrity as, above all, "Apostle" and, then necessarily, as "Apostle of the Gentiles" (Gal 1:16; Rom 11:13; 15:16).

Hence the questions for this chapter. How must we critically assess Luke-Acts on Paul—especially in terms of Peter? What does Luke-Acts intend by emphasizing—or inventing—so many parallels between Peter and Paul, parallels that do not exalt Paul beside Peter but locate Paul below Peter? What was it especially, specifically, and particularly about the historical and factual Paul that persuaded or forced Luke-Acts to invent the apologetical and fictional Paul? How does Peter rather than Paul support Roman rather than Jewish Christianity as Luke-Acts' vision of the Messianic/Christic future?

Parallel Beginnings

The apostles pivot from the first to the second volume of *The Gospel according to Luke-Acts* in Jerusalem and its Temple (Luke 24:53; Acts 2:46). Then, in Acts, at Jerusalem, and among the apostles, Peter stands out repeatedly. He is named first among them (1:13), speaks authoritatively both to them (1:15) and for them (2:14,37; 5:29). He is named with "Peter and John" but always in that order (3:1,3,11; 4:1,13,19). Also, when together, it is Peter and not John who speaks (3:4,6,12; 4:8). Finally, it is Peter alone who acts on the case of Ananias and Sapphira (5:1–11).

It is not at all surprising that the post-Easter life of Peter begins very publicly in Jerusalem. What is surprising and significant is that Luke-Acts goes out of its way to have Paul's public life also begin in Jerusalem. By contrast—and contradiction—when Paul himself described his first visit to Jerusalem after his vocation-revelation, he declared: "In what I am writing to you, before God, I do not lie! . . . I was still unknown by sight to the churches of Judea that are in Christ; they only heard it said, 'The one who formerly was persecuting us is now proclaiming the faith he once tried to destroy'" (Gal 1:20,22–23). Paul's public life began not in Jerusalem but in Damascus—note that "returned to Damascus" (Gal 1:17). Here, however, is how Acts describes and emphasizes repeatedly that, while Peter began in Jerusalem as an apostle persecuted by the high-priests (4:1,23; 5:24), Paul began in Jerusalem as a persecutor accredited by those same high-priests.

First, for Acts, Paul's public career starts in Jerusalem as a semi-persecutor at the murder of Stephen: "they dragged him [Stephen] out of the city and began to stone him; and the witnesses laid their coats at the feet of a young man named Saul . . . and Saul approved of their killing him" (Acts 7:58; 8:1). Later, again in Jerusalem, Paul "fell into a trance" while praying in the Temple and confessed to a visionary Jesus that "'while the blood of your witness Stephen was shed, I myself was standing by, approving and keeping the coats of those who killed him'" (22:20; and note 22:22!). That is simply a Lukan fiction to associate Paul with Stephen's death not as a stone-thrower but as a coat-watcher!

Next, Acts places this admission of his inaugural but much fuller persecution in Jerusalem on Paul's lips to the Roman authorities at Caesarea Maritima:

> I myself was convinced that I ought to do many things against the name of Jesus of Nazareth. And that is what I did in Jerusalem; with authority received from the chief priests, I not only locked up many of the saints in prison, but I also cast my vote against them when they were being condemned to death. By punishing them often in all the synagogues I tried to force them to blaspheme. (26:9–11a)

Notice that Paul's authority as a persecutor in Jerusalem derived from the highest Jewish authority there and against the earliest Messianic/ Christic members there.

Finally, for Acts, it was because of the Lukan-Paul's murderous success as a persecutor in Jerusalem that those same authorities gave him written power to take dissidents in Damascus back to Jerusalem:

> Saul . . . went to the high priest and asked him for letters to the synagogues at Damascus, so that if he found any who belonged to the Way, men or women, he might bring them bound to Jerusalem. (9:1–2)
>
> From them [the high priest and the whole council of elders] I also received letters to the brothers in Damascus, and I went there in order to bind those who were there and to bring them back to Jerusalem for punishment. (22:5b)
>
> I was so furiously enraged at them, I pursued them even to foreign cities. (26:11b)

That, bluntly, is not even good historical fiction: the high priest had no authority to administer the death penalty even in Jerusalem under a Roman procurator/prefect; and a high priest had absolutely no authority from Jerusalem to Damascus, in Damascus, or from Damascus back to Jerusalem.

If we only had those parallel beginnings between Peter and Paul in Jerusalem, we might see them as part of Luke's plan to start everything in and from Jerusalem: "you will be my witnesses in Jerusalem, in all Judea and Samaria, and to the ends of the earth" (Acts 1:8). Starting Paul in Jerusalem might be an innocent Lukan fiction—except for how those parallels continue to their climax over the next two steps.

Parallel Events

Here are multiple events that happen to Peter and Paul but always first to Peter and then to Paul:

> *Speeches* about Jesus the Messiah/Christ: *first,* by Peter to Jews at Jerusalem (2:14–36) and to Gentiles at coastal Caesarea (10:34–43); and, *then,* by Paul to Jews at Pisidian Antioch (13:16–41) and to Gentiles at Athens (17:22–31). Also, to emphasize the parallelism, Luke-Acts divides each of those speeches to fellow Jews into three parts by repeated addresses to the audience.
>
> *Healings* of a man lame "from birth" by "looking at him intently" and commanding him to "stand": *first,* by Peter (3:1–10) and, *then,* by Paul (14:8–10);
>
> *Exorcisms* of demons: *first,* by Peter (5:16) and, *then,* by Paul (16:16–18);
>
> *Escapes* from prison by miracle: *first,* by Peter (5:17–26) and, *then,* by Paul (16:25–39);
>
> *Defeats* of a "magician": *first,* by Peter (8:17–24) and, *then,* by Paul (13:8–11);
>
> *Raisings* of the dead: *first,* by Peter (9:36–43) and, *then,* by Paul (20:7–12); both start "in a room upstairs" and both become "alive."

It is hard to survey that sequence without wondering if the Lukan-Paul is anything other than a Peter-come-lately, a second-hand version of somebody much more important who preceded him in event after event. And that process gets worse.

Parallel Vocations

Among all such parallel events between Peter and Paul, this is by far the most important one. Peter and Paul have vocation-revelations with regard to Gentile membership in the Messianic/Christic community. Both experiences are told three times, rather than simply told once and then referenced summarily twice. They both also vary in this same way:

> *Peter's* vocation-revelation is first told in Luke-Acts as it happens at Joppa (10:1–48) and is then retold twice by the Lukan Peter to his fellow apostles in Jerusalem (11:4–18; 15:7–11). In those first two accounts, the vocation takes place as Peter "heard a voice saying" (10:13; 11:7).
>
> *Paul's* vocation-revelation is first told in Luke-Acts as it happens in Damascus (9:3:19a) and is then retold twice by the Lukan-Paul to a Jewish audience at Jerusalem (22:6–21) and a Gentile audience at Caesarea Maritima (26:12–18). And, once again, but now three times, the vocation takes place as Paul "heard a voice saying" (9:4; 22:7; 26:14).

Still, as Luke-Acts creates that ascendancy of Peter over Paul, there are three gestures toward the historical accuracy of the opposite reality, three confirmations—if such are needed—that Acts knows exactly what it is doing and does it quite deliberately.

First, at least Paul's divine vocation gets a mention first in Acts 9 immediately before Peter's in Acts 10. Second, and more significantly, as the Lukan-Paul retells his Damascus experience to inimical fellow Jews in Jerusalem, he suddenly switches from Ananias speaking to him in Damascus to Jesus speaking to him in Jerusalem:

> After I had returned to Jerusalem and while I was praying in the temple, I fell into a trance and saw Jesus saying to me, "Hurry and get out of Jerusalem quickly, because they will not accept your testimony about me." And I said, "Lord, they themselves know that in every synagogue I imprisoned and beat those who believed in you. And while

> the blood of your witness Stephen was shed, I myself
> was standing by, approving and keeping the coats of those
> who killed him." Then he said to me, "Go, for I will send
> you far away to the Gentiles." (22:17–21)

That is actually the conclusion to Paul's vocation-revelation account
but now transposed from Damascus to Jerusalem and its Temple.
But, more importantly, that final sentence is the closest Luke-Acts
ever comes to agreeing with Paul that his vocation-revelation was—
specially and particularly, theoretically and practically—"that I might
proclaim him [God's Son] among the Gentiles" (Gal 1:16).

Finally, Luke's version of the so-called Jerusalem Conference
is communal, orderly, and serenely peaceful. (Later, we will have to
compare this in detail with Paul's rather less peaceful version.) In
Acts 15, the meeting in Jerusalem was necessitated when "some
believers who belonged to the sect of the Pharisees stood up and
said, 'It is necessary for them to be circumcised and ordered to keep
the law of Moses'" (Acts 15:5). Watch, then the juxtaposition and
sequence that follows:

> After there had been much debate, Peter stood up and
> said to them, "My brothers, you know that in the early
> days God made a choice among you, that I should be the
> one through whom the Gentiles would hear the message
> of the good news and become believers." (15:7)
>
> The whole assembly kept silence, and listened to Barn-
> abas and Paul as they told of all the signs and wonders
> that God had done through them among the Gentiles.
> (15:12)

Acts has Peter speak first and he gets five verses of direct quotation
(15:7–11). Then, and only then, "Barnabas and Paul" (note order) get
one verse and not in direct speech (15:12).

James, the brother of Jesus, gives the final decision in favor of
the Gentile admission free of circumcision—in nine verses of direct
quotation (15:13–21). But, ignoring "Barnabas and Paul," he recalls
only that "Simeon [Peter] has related how God first looked favorably
on the Gentiles, to take from among them a people for his name"

(15:14). That decision is then recorded in a letter that is cited verbatim as if it were taken from archival records. In that letter, "Barnabas and Paul" are mentioned, but so are "Judas and Silas" and they seem much more significant:

> We have decided unanimously to choose representatives and send them to you [Gentiles], along with our beloved Barnabas and Paul, who have risked their lives for the sake of our Lord Jesus Christ. We have therefore sent Judas and Silas, who themselves will tell you the same things by word of mouth . . . Judas and Silas, who were themselves prophets, said much to encourage and strengthen the believers. (15:25–27,32)

If you read Acts 15, and knew nothing else, you would conclude that James and Peter were very important, that Judas and Silas were important, and that Barnabas and Paul were—at the most—also present.

In summary. Luke-Acts' insistent exaltation of Peter over Paul and especially its creation of Peter rather than Paul as the Apostle of the Gentiles is later apologetical interpretation rather than earlier historical information. But, actually, the situation is even worse as Luke-Acts presents it: Paul could never have been the "Apostle of the Gentiles" because Paul was not even an "apostle." For that, we travel one final time "on the road to Damascus" with the Lukan-Paul.

—————————◆—————————

As just seen, Luke-Acts has three accounts of Paul's vocation-revelation but varies that repetition in two ways to avoid literary redundancy. First, with regard to Paul's audience, that story is told: about Paul, as biography in the third person (Acts 9:3–19a); by Paul, as autobiography in the first person, to "the people" in Jerusalem (22:6–21); and again by Paul, as autobiography in the first person, to the Roman authorities at coastal Caesarea (26:12–18).

Next, with regard to Paul's destiny, that role is told by God to Ananias in Damascus (9:15–16); by Ananias to Paul in Damascus (22:14–15); and by God to Paul on the road to Damascus—with

Ananias not even mentioned (26:16–18). That allows for a climactic build-up across the three versions. After Jesus and his parables, Luke-Acts is the best teller of tales in the New Testament—but, of course, tales, like parables, can be fictions.

Despite those literary variations and rhetorical modifications across its three accounts, Luke-Acts kept one section strikingly the same. It is the unchanging core of the event—for the Lukan-Paul. That core involved light and voice, question and response—in all three versions:

> Suddenly a light from heaven flashed around him. He fell to the ground and heard a voice saying to him, "Saul, Saul, why do you persecute me?" He asked, "Who are you, Lord?" The reply came, "I am Jesus, whom you are persecuting." (9:3–5)
>
> About noon a great light from heaven suddenly shone about me. I fell to the ground and heard a voice saying to me, "Saul, Saul, why are you persecuting me?" I answered, "Who are you, Lord?" Then he said to me, "I am Jesus of Nazareth whom you are persecuting." (22:6–8)
>
> At midday along the road, your Excellency, I saw a light from heaven, brighter than the sun, shining around me and my companions. When we had all fallen to the ground, I heard a voice saying to me in the Hebrew language, "Saul, Saul, why are you persecuting me? It hurts you to kick against the goads." I asked, "Who are you, Lord?" The Lord answered, "I am Jesus whom you are persecuting." (26:12–15)

First, the Lukan-Paul did not see a vision of Jesus but of a light strong enough to knock him to the ground. Next, he did not even recognize the voice he heard and had to ask its identity. Finally, lest there be any mistake, he could not have seen Jesus since he was blinded completely by the light. That theme is repeated three times in the first account:

> Saul got up from the ground, and though his eyes were open, he could see nothing; so they led him by the hand

and brought him into Damascus. For three days he was without sight, and neither ate nor drank. (9:8–9)

[Paul had] "seen in a vision a man named Ananias come in and lay his hands on him so that he might regain his sight." (9:12)

Ananias . . . laid his hands on Saul and said, "Brother Saul, the Lord Jesus, who appeared to you on your way here, has sent me so that you may regain your sight and be filled with the Holy Spirit." And immediately something like scales fell from his eyes, and his sight was restored. Then he got up and was baptized. (9:17–18=22:11,13)

That is a classic description of a visionary trance and might seem a legitimate dramatization of what Paul himself described to the Galatians as an "apocalyptic revelation" (Gal 1:12,16). Also, Paul's pre-baptismal blindness and post-baptismal sight presented a powerful model for all future Messianic/Christic converts. Finally, Paul's release from blindness in those first two accounts makes him the perfect embodiment of the vocation given to him directly by God in the third account: "'I will rescue you from your people and from the Gentiles—to whom I am sending you to open their eyes so that they may turn from darkness to light'" (26:17–18).

Still, the Lukan-Paul did not and could not *see* Jesus since he was blinded by the light. In fact, he did not even recognize his voice ("Who are you?"). What happened to Paul on the Damascus road was not an ecstatic vision (from Latin *videre*, to see) but an ecstatic audition (from Latin *audire*, to hear). For Luke, Paul could never claim to be an apostle equal to the Twelve who had both *seen* Jesus and been *sent* by him—from Greek *apostellein*, to send—both before (Luke 6:13) and after his resurrection (Acts 1:3,8).

Furthermore, since the Lukan-Paul is not an apostle, how could he be the Apostle "among the Gentiles" (Gal 1:16)? Watch how Luke-Acts described the vocation of Paul across the three accounts of that destiny—the Gentiles are certainly mentioned but so are the Jews:

> *Jesus to Ananias:* "Go, for he [Paul] is an instrument whom I have chosen to bring my name before Gentiles

and kings and before the people of Israel; I myself will
show him how much he must suffer for the sake of my
name." (9:15–16)

Ananias to Paul: "The God of our ancestors has chosen
you to know his will, to see the Righteous One and to hear
his own voice; for you will be his witness to all the world
of what you have seen and heard." (22:12–15)

Jesus to Paul: "I will rescue you from your people and
from the Gentiles—to whom I am sending *(apostello)* you
to open their eyes so that they may turn from darkness to
light . . . [since] the Messiah . . . would proclaim light both
to our people and to the Gentiles." (26:17–18,23)

For Luke, Paul's destiny is to "Gentiles and kings and . . . the people
of Israel" or "to all the world." Even in that last account, when the
Lukan-Paul is *sent* to the Gentiles, that accurate record is framed by a
double mention of "your/our people" and the "Gentiles."

———·····∙∙∙∎∎∎∎∎∎∎✦∎∎∎∎∎∎∙∙∙·····———

So much for Luke-Acts, but what about Paul himself? First,
he recognized that, unlike the Twelve, he himself had never seen
the *earthly* Jesus. So, he dismissed their advantage rather truculently:
"From now on, therefore, we regard no one from a human point of
view; even though we once knew Christ from a human point of view,
we know him no longer in that way" (2 Cor 5:16).

Paul, however, insists repeatedly that, at his vocation-revelation
he had both seen and heard the heavenly Jesus and that made him
equal in authority to the Twelve in Jerusalem. He asked rhetorically:
"Am I not an apostle? Have I not seen Jesus our Lord?" (1 Cor 9:1).
More pointedly, recall this series:

Christ . . . appeared to Cephas, then to the Twelve. Then
he appeared to more than five hundred. . . .Then he appeared to James, then to all the apostles. Last of all, as to
one untimely born, he appeared also to me. For I am the
least of the apostles, unfit to be called an apostle, because
I persecuted the church of God. (1 Cor 15:3–9)

That word "appeared" (*ōphthē*) is a Greek passive meaning literally "was seen to." Although a vision of the heavenly Jesus is not enough to make one an apostle, it is a necessary condition for the call that may accompany it. Thus Paul can be the last, the least, and the most unfit apostle, but that makes him still an apostle just like the other ones. In fact, he can almost offhandedly refer to the other apostles as simply "those who were already apostles before me" (Gal 1:17). Those others had priority in time but not priority in authority.

Paul also insisted on that apostolic authority in the opening of several letters: "Paul, called to be an apostle of Christ Jesus by the will of God" (1 Cor 1:1) and again "Paul, an apostle of Christ Jesus by the will of God" (2 Cor 1:1). But when that apostolic authority was itself in question, the letter began authoritatively and polemically: "Paul an apostle—sent neither by human commission nor from human authorities, but through Jesus Christ and God the Father, who raised him from the dead" (Gal 1:1). Also, Paul, as we saw in his own vocation description, is not just another apostle but one called specifically to proclaim the Son of God "among the Gentiles" (Gal 1:16).

Finally, the majestic opening for the epistle to the Romans begins: "Paul, a servant of Jesus Christ, called to be an apostle, set apart for the gospel of God . . . through whom we have received grace and apostleship . . . among all the Gentiles . . . including yourselves" (1:1, 5–6). Paul both saw and heard the heavenly Jesus and was called through that combination to become an apostle specifically "among the Gentiles" (Gal 1:16), "to the Gentiles" (Rom 11:13), and, more solemnly and climactically, "to be a minister of Christ Jesus to the Gentiles in the priestly service of the gospel of God, so that the offering of the Gentiles may be acceptable, sanctified by the Holy Spirit" (Rom 15:16).

In summary. Paul himself made three claims about the apocalypse that consummated his vocation-revelation experience: he both saw and heard the heavenly Jesus; he was called and sent as an apostle; he was "separated apart" as a/the apostle "among the Gentiles." The Paul of Luke-Acts contradicts all three claims: Paul only heard but did not see Jesus; he was not called as an independent apostle but as a dependent missionary; his mission was to both Jews and Gentiles and not specifically for the latter.

What is the authorial purpose for that stunning divergence between the Pauline and Lukan versions of Paul's vocation-story? Why does Luke-Acts negate Paul as an Apostle and thereby, of course, deny his status as Apostle of the Gentiles? Why transfer Paul's revelation, vocation, and mission from Paul to Peter in Acts? Why that quite deliberate denigration of Paul and exaltation of Peter?

Think of what we have already seen of Paul's powerful combination of both his earlier Pharisaic and later Messianic/Christic faiths. Think about the radicalism of his vision of universal resurrection, general judgment, and eternal recompense as a present in-time process with God rather than just as a future end-time product by God. Think of his challenge that followers of Jesus the Messiah/Christ live within that process and thereby create its reality, thereby validate its truth, thereby participate in God's present "justification" of the world.

Paul as a Messianic/Christic-Pharisee affronted fellow Pharisees by being a Messianic/Christic one, affronted fellow Messianic/Christics by being a Pharisee, and affronted Romans—if they had read him—for his alternative program to their own imperial "justification" of the world (Rom 4:15; 5:16,18, 21). Paul was simply too radical for them all then—and for us now?—and needed already to be deradicalized and reRomanized—even within the New Testament itself.

Since Paul had already written his radical vision into history with his authentic seven letters, you could deradicalize him in three main written ways: by counter-insertions in the original letters of Paul the Apostle; by counter-letters written in the name of "Paul the Apostle"; and, climactically as in Luke-Acts, by negating his very status as Paul the Apostle. In other words, what Luke-Acts did to Paul was but the climax of a deradicalization process already operational by the early second century.

Here is one example of such an insertion and it parallels that apologetical ascendancy of Peter over Paul just seen in Acts. The

New Testament contains two letters fictionally attributed to Peter. In the first letter, pseudo-Peter commands,

> For the Lord's sake accept the authority of every human institution, whether of the emperor as supreme, or of governors, as sent by him to punish those who do wrong and to praise those who do right. . . . Honor the emperor. (1 Peter 2:13–17)

The "emperor" is simply called "king" (*basileus*) which reminds us that "the kingdom of God" is what Roman Imperial Theology could have called its own empire! Also, that traditional Roman hierarchy of rulers over subjects (2:13–17) continues into owners over slaves (2:18–25) and husbands over wives (3:1–7).

Hold that in mind as I turn next to the most controversial text ever written by Paul if, in fact, it was so written. I give it in full so you can see that it is not a passing comment or throwaway line but a pounded-out injunction:

> Let every person be subject to the governing authorities; for there is no authority except from God, and those authorities that exist have been instituted by God. Therefore whoever resists authority resists what God has appointed, and those who resist will incur judgment. For rulers (*archontes*) are not a terror to good conduct, but to bad. Do you wish to have no fear of the authority? Then do what is good, and you will receive its approval; for it is God's servant for your good. But if you do what is wrong, you should be afraid, for the authority does not bear the sword in vain! It is the servant of God to execute wrath on the wrongdoer. Therefore one must be subject, not only because of wrath but also because of conscience. For the same reason you also pay taxes, for the authorities are God's servants, busy with this very thing. Pay to all what is due them—taxes to whom taxes are due, revenue to whom revenue is due, respect to whom respect is due, honor to whom honor is due. (Rom 13:1–7)

The major question is whether that text came originally and authentically from Paul in writing Romans or was inserted very early by later tradition from that same just-seen-pseudo-Petrine text or at least from the attitude behind it.

First, I am reluctant to answer affirmatively because, with most scholars, claiming an insertion seems like a dishonest solution to a disliked text. Yet short of a temporary loss of Pauline nerve, thought, or mind, I simply cannot reconcile that statement about "rulers" (*archontes*) in Rom 13:3 with the only other time Paul uses that term:

> Among the mature we do speak wisdom, though it is not a wisdom of this age or of the rulers (*archontes*) of this age, who are doomed to perish. . . . None of the rulers (*archontes*) of this age understood this; for if they had, they would not have crucified the Lord of glory. (1 Cor 2:6,8)

I conclude, therefore, that Rom 13:1–7 is a post-, pseudo-, and anti-Pauline insertion not because I do not like it but because Paul did not write it.

Second, as has often been noted, if you omit Rom 13:1–7, you can read smoothly from the immediately preceding 12:14–21 into the immediately succeeding 13:8–10. But that continuity can be specified more precisely. Those two sections are the closest Paul ever came to repeating the most radical teachings of Jesus by starting them with, "Bless those who persecute you; bless and do not curse them" (12:14) and ending with, "Love does no wrong to a neighbor; therefore, love is the fulfilling of the law" (13:10). That recalls rather closely Jesus' injunction from the Sermon on the Mount to "Love your enemies and pray for those who persecute you" (Matt 5:44) or to "Love your enemies, do good to those who hate you, bless those who curse you, pray for those who abuse you" (Luke 6:27–28).

Third, this is what I imagine to have happened. In Romans, Paul continued consecutively from 12:14–21 into 13:8–10. A later scribe or tradition noted Paul's command, "To nobody evil for evil repaying" (12:17, literally) and its similarity to, "Not repaying evil for evil" (1 Pet 3:9a, literally). Since Peter combined that phrase with obedience to imperial hierarchy, 13:1–7 was inserted forcibly into

Romans so that Paul made the same conjunction of life inside and outside the community.

Finally, to continue the damage control of fictional Peter on historical Paul, there is this rather ambiguous comment about the necessity of "patience":

> So also our beloved brother Paul wrote to you according to the wisdom given him, speaking of this as he does in all his letters. There are some things in them hard to understand, which the ignorant and unstable twist to their own destruction, as they do the other scriptures. (2 Pet 3:15–16)

All in all, therefore, I think Rom 13:1–7 is best seen as an insertion *after* Paul rather than an injunction *from* Paul and that it comes from Peter into Paul and 1 Peter 3 into Romans 13. It is, however, only one such post-Pauline deradicalization of the historical Paul. Next comes another and even wider one—not by insertion within an original Pauline letter but by the creation of multiple post-Pauline letters.

———————————————✦———————————————

As we saw already, there is a general scholarly consensus that six of the letters attributed to Paul are probably (Colossians, Ephesians, 2 Thessalonians) or certainly (1–2 Timothy, Titus) pseudo- or even anti-Pauline texts. That post-Pauline tradition to deradicalize Paul's vision worked by reaffirming exactly what he had negated and by restoring the three representative ascendances that he had annulled.

Paul—to be seen more fully later—had negated the validity of the standard religio-political and socio-economic hierarchies of Greeks over Jews, frees over slaves (1 Cor 12:13) or, more fully, of Greek over Jew, free over slave, and male over female (Gal 3:28). Watch, then, how those latter two negations are counter negated, that is, reaffirmed by the post-, pseudo-, and anti-Pauline tradition that writes in the name of Paul the apostle.

First, Paul's negation of "slave or free" is firmly annulled in the later pseudo-Pauline letters. They take intra-Christian slavery totally for granted and specify only that Christian masters be "kind" to their

slaves and Christian slaves be "obedient" to their masters. For the
former, their model is "the Master in Heaven." For the latter, their
"inheritance" is in heaven (Col 3:22–4:1; Eph 6:6–9).

Next, Paul's negation of "male and female" is equally annulled
in those same two pseudo-Pauline letters. They take the ascendancy
of male over female in husband over wife totally for granted and
specify only that Christian husbands be loving and Christian wives
be subject: "Wives, be subject to your husbands, as is fitting in the
Lord. Husbands, love your wives and never treat them harshly" (Col
3:18–19; Eph 5:22–33).

Still, in those consensually-probable post-Pauline letters, Paul
at least addressed both parties directly. He spoke to both slaves and
masters, wives and husbands. He told each that they had mutual even
if unequal responsibilities under Christ.

Finally, however, in the consensually-certain post-Pauline letters,
both parties of masters/slaves or husbands/wives are not addressed
but only the masters or husbands in each case. Also, there is no mention of mutual responsibilities. As forgeries, those letters are more reactionary than conservative with regard to the historical Paul. Thus, for
example, pseudo-Paul now says to Timothy that, "I permit no woman
to teach or to have authority over a man; she is to keep silent" (1 Tim
2:12); and to Titus, "Tell slaves to be submissive to their masters and to
give satisfaction in every respect; they are not to talk back" (Titus 2:9).

——·····•:◻:◻:◆:◻:◻:•·····——

All of those just-mentioned conservative post-Pauline letters
open from Paul "an apostle of Christ Jesus" and the reactionary ones
have Paul cite himself as "appointed a herald and an apostle" (1 Tim
2:7; 2 Tim 1:11). Their solution for Pauline deradicalization is to have
their fictional Paul negate undesirable aspects of the historical Paul's
emphasis on the cosmic justice demanded by baptismal rebirth.

Still, for those pseudo-Pauline letters, he was always an "apostle" and indeed even one to and of the Gentiles: "Although I am
the very least of all the saints, this grace was given to me to bring to
the Gentiles the news of the boundless riches of Christ" (Eph 3:8);
again, "For this I was appointed a herald and an apostle (I am telling

the truth, I am not lying), a teacher of the Gentiles in faith and truth" (1 Tim 2:7).

Luke-Acts, however, goes far beyond the Pauline deradicalization of those pseudo-letters with a pseudo-narrative that makes Paul a great missionary to Jews and Gentiles but not especially, particularly, exclusively, an Apostle to the Gentiles. Indeed, the very opening of Acts rules out even the possibility of Paul as an Apostle equal to the Twelve. There, as Peter—of course!—proclaimed, the replacement for Judas had to be, "one of the men (*andrōn*) who have accompanied us during all the time that the Lord Jesus went in and out among us, beginning from the baptism of John until the day when he was taken up from us—one of these must become a witness with us to his resurrection" (Acts 1:21–22). Paul was excluded as an apostle before he even entered the story or text of Luke-Acts.

In summary. Already within the New Testament, the post-Pauline tradition is a carefully crafted denigration of the historical Paul as a Messianic/Christic Pharisee. Thereby, it certifies the profound radicality—and ultimate cosmic validity—of his vision.

Chapter 5

"I WENT AWAY AT ONCE
INTO ARABIA"

Arabia entered upon a golden age of Nabatean civilization under the leadership of the long-lived monarch Aretas IV. . . .
The resplendent rule of Aretas gave stability to the adjacent
realm of the Nabateans. . . . [He] was the most prolific minter
of Nabatean coins in the kingdom's history . . . eight of every
ten known Nabatean coins are of Aretas IV ... unprecedented
prosperity and growth of the Nabatean kingdom during the
long years of his reign. . . . undoubtedly one of the greatest
figures in the history of pre-Islamic Arabia.

—Glen W. Bowersock, *Roman Arabia*

In the last decade before the Common Era, the axis of power on
the Jordan River slipped—slowly but surely—from west-bank Jewish
Herodians to east-bank Arab Nabateans. The first sign of that shift
appeared with the new Nabatean monarch, Aretas IV Philopatris,
who ruled between 8 BCE and 40 CE from his capital at Petra, famously described by the English biblical scholar John William Burgon—
who had not yet been there—as "a rose-red city half as old as time."
    Aretas IV's regnal title was used over fifty years earlier by Are-
tas III who had ruled from 87 to 62 BCE. He had conquered the Transjordanian reaches as far north as Damascus, where he struck bronze
coins between 84 and 72 BCE. Also, Aretas IV's personal honorific,
Philopatris, lover of his people, presumably promised them something special—maybe even Damascus once again? (Aretas III's honorific was a more general Philhellene.) In any case, hold that potential
future for a moment to meet Aretas' people, the Nabateans of Arabia.
    In the latter half of the first century BCE, the Greek historian
Diodorus of Sicily wrote that, "while there are many Arabian tribes

who use the desert as pasture, the Nabataeans far surpass the others in wealth. . . . [They] bring down to the sea frankincense and myrrh and the most valuable kinds of spices, which they procure from those who convey them from what is called Arabia Eudaemon" (*Universal History* 19.94.5). Greek *Arabia Eudaemon,* or Roman *Arabia Felix,* is modern Yemen at the southern tip of Saudi Arabia.

By the first century CE, Nabatean power was based on their skill in sailing the Red Sea with lateen-rigged ships, crossing the desert with camel caravans, and deliberately misleading an invading Roman army almost to extinction when it—most unwisely—chose Nabatean desert guides. Nabatean prosperity was based on controlling and even monopolizing commerce in spices and perfumes, gems and metals, frankincense and myrrh, obsidian and bitumen northward and westward from the Arabian Peninsula into Rome's Mediterranean globalization.

At that same time, however, the Nabateans were also becoming a sedentary, urban, and even territorially imperial people. Apart from his primary capital at Petra in southern Transjordan, Aretas IV had a secondary one at Bosra in norther Transjordan. From Petra to Bosra is 217 miles but from Bosra to Damascus is only 85. In terms of cities, at Bosra, Aretas IV was already almost to Damascus. By 8 BCE, therefore, the eastern side of the Jordan was united under a single strong ruler and poised for regional greatness. By contrast, from 4 BCE onward, the western side was disunited under multiple weak rulers—Roman and/or Herodian—and poised for regional disaster.

That disastrous future started with the emperor Caesar Augustus' geopolitical blunder in solving the problem of the Herodian succession. To be fair, Augustus made few such major political mistakes but this one would have tragic results both for his Jewish subjects and his own Julio-Claudian dynasty.

In the spring of 4 BCE the seventy-year-old Herod the Great—who makes Henry the Eighth look both monogamous and magnanimous—was already on his death-bed in the winter palace at Jericho. A few years earlier he had executed for treason two of his three older sons and, in his last week, he also executed Antipater, his eldest son and heir apparent. That left only the three younger sons, Archelaus, Philip II, and Antipas as potential heirs. When he changed his will after Antipater's death, the dying Herod "named Antipas king, passing over his eldest [remaining] sons, Archelaus and Philip" (*JW* 1.646=*JA* 17.146). But then, even in his death-throes, he "changed his mind, . . . once more altered his will and designated Antipas, to whom he had left his throne, to be tetrarch of Galilee and Peraea, while he bestowed the kingdom on Archelaus," and gave the Transjordanian territories in the far north to Philip II (*JW* 1.664–669=*JA* 17.188–189). In other words, half of Antipas' tetrarchy—Peraea—and all of Philip's were located *east* of the Jordan. And, there, Aretas IV watched—and waited.

All of that was, of course, subject to Roman consent, and Augustus, accepting Herod's final will, divided his kingdom among those three younger sons but with Archelaus not as monarch (sole ruler) but only as ethnarch (people leader). That decision was, however, initially so complicated that, to decide it, Augustus convened a solemn council in the Temple of Apollo adjoining his home on the Palatine Hill in Rome.

That complication came from an alternative solution to the problem of the Herodian succession. A delegation of "fifty" Jews from Jerusalem along with "eight thousand" Jews from Rome were backed by Herod's relatives—especially his sister Salome—as well as some of the Syrian authorities in pleading three strongly alternative choices for the Herodian succession. Their first choice was to annul the monarchy and make Israel an ethnic enclave fully within the Roman province of Syria and directly under its proconsular governor. Failing that, their second choice was to make Antipas king. Finally, if both those options were unacceptable, never, ever make Archelaus the ruler! (*JW* 2.80=*JA* 17.300).

To my mind, Augustus should have accepted full Syrian incorporation because, while we can never know how that would have worked out, it could hardly have been worse than what happened with the disastrous revolt against Rome in 66–74 CE. Then, as Tacitus put it, "The Jews' patience lasted until Gessius Florus became procurator [64–66]: in his time war began" (*Histories* 5.9–10). In any case, Augustus honored Herod's final will, divided the country between his youngest sons and, with that mistake, set the stage for ultimate tragedy.

In summary. At the start of the Common Era, therefore, a single strong king ruled east of the Jordan and weak Herodian princes or Roman sub-governors ruled to its west. Worse still, Augustus had given Antipas half his tetrarchy and Philip II all of his not to the west but to the east of the river. To relocate and rephrase Tacitus: the patience of Aretas IV lasted until the early 30s: at that time war began.

One final quote from Bowersock on Roman Arabia: "for about the first thirty years of the Christian era, Aretas was in a position to lead his nation in relative peace. It was only in the final decade of his life that serious troubles are known to have arisen" (page 60). But that "final decade of his life" was the 30s and it was precisely in those years that Paul "went away into Arabia" (Gal 1:17) and fell afoul at Damascus of its "governor under King Aretas" (2 Cor 11:32). Paul's Arabian Mission was doomed, as we shall see, to unfortunate and almost fatal failure: he was the wrong person, in the wrong place, at the wrong time, for the wrong reason.

Paul records his first or Arabian Mission with an ultra-terse comment about what happened immediately after his vocation-revelation in Damascus: "I went away at once into Arabia, and afterwards I returned to Damascus" (Gal 1:17b). Called to proclaim God's Son "among the Gentiles" Paul goes "immediately to "Arabia"—but why Arabia, where in Arabia, and what happened in Arabia?

Paul went to the Nabateans in "Arabia" as the obvious place to begin his commission since those "Gentiles" had Abrahamic ancestry, adjacent geography, male circumcision, and similar language— with Nabatean as a dialect of Aramaic. But where exactly did Paul go among the Nabatean Arabs, where precisely was the focus of his "Arabia"?

To answer we must resist having our imagination totally dominated by exotic Petra, that extraordinary Nabatean capital in southern Transjordan. It is romantically seductive to imagine Paul entering Petra through its three-quarter-mile-long, high-walled, and narrow passageway. But for Paul's Arabian Mission, I think much less about

Petra and much more about Bosra—modern Busra al-Sham in south-ernmost Syria, to the east of the Sea of Galilee. As we saw above, that fort city in the north was, by the time of Aretas IV, a secondary capital to primary Petra in the south. Bosra, in fact, was significant enough that, when the Romans established the province of Arabia in 106 CE, they made Bosra not Petra its capital and stationed a legion there.

(In 1965 to 1967, during post-doctorate study in Jerusalem—then in Jordan—my every visitor wanted to see Petra so I got there about a half-dozen times. But nobody mentioned Bosra/Busra. I got there only once on the way from Jerusalem to Damascus and, to my present chagrin, I was actually more interested in nearby Deraa and what happened there in T. E. Lawrence's *Seven Pillars of Wisdom*, which I was then reading. Both Petra and Bosra are now World Heritage sites.)

First, remember that the Jordan valley is a fault line between the Arabian and African tectonic plates. It forms a northern sliver of the Great Rift Valley which in its entirety makes the Grand Canyon look like a large ditch. Due east of the Sea of Galilee is the Hauran which is a region of volcanic hills, lava fields, and basalt layers. Also, however, its location south of the Lebanon mountains allowed Mediterranean rainfall to escape inland and produce fertile fields that fed runoffs into the Yarmuk river as it emptied westward to the Jordan.

Next, based on that geography, the Middle Eastern archaeologist Warwick Ball[1] wrote:

> The Hauran is an extraordinary landscape. . . . Astonishingly, this area of volcanic desolation is interspersed with abundant, rich agricultural land and settlement, and has almost more ancient remains than anywhere else in the Middle East—the remains of some three hundred ancient towns and villages have been counted in the Hauran. For the volcanic eruptions which produced the basalt also produced a highly fertile soil in the valleys and plains not

---

[1] Warwick Ball, *Syria: A Historical and Architectural Guide*. Northampton, MA: Interlink Books, 2007.

covered by the lava flows, making it one of the Near East's main granaries in antiquity. (page 85)

Finally, then, my proposal for Paul's "Arabia" is that he focused on the Hauran and used Bosra as his winter base. On the one hand, that gave him access to Nabatean "Gentiles" in settled towns and villages but within what was also a crossroads for desert caravans between Egypt and Syria, Arabia and the Mediterranean. On the other hand, the Hauran was within the territories of Herod Philip II—with Bosra outside but near its southern border—and that may have supplied some Jewish protection for Paul. At the start of what he described to the Galatians as "three years" in "Arabia," all must have looked supremely hopeful for Paul's first mission "among the Gentiles." What then went so terribly wrong that Paul himself summarized—or even negated—that mission with this terse line: "I went away at once into Arabia, and afterwards I returned to Damascus"? Come back, as you probably expect by now, to Aretas IV Philopatris, king of the Nabatean Arabs, but based now on Bowersock's interpretation of Aretas' territorial designs and imperial plans (pages 65–69).

—·····⋯⋯⋯✦⋯⋯·····—

According to Josephus, there was already "the start of a quarrel" between Antipas and Aretas in 28 CE when, in order to marry Herodias, Antipas repudiated his Nabatean wife, the princess Phasaelis, daughter of Aretas IV (*JA* 18.109–112). But that political tension became a territorial conflict when Herod Philip II died in 34 CE and Aretas invaded his territory. Antipas opposed him, and, "in that dispute about boundaries in the district of Gamla . . . [Antipas'] whole army was destroyed when some refugees, who had come from the tetrarchy of Philip, and had joined Herod's army, played him false" (*JA* 18.113–114).

At Gamla, Aretas was already fighting north of Antipas' Perean territory, north of the Decapolis cities, north even of his own fortress city of Bosra, and deep inside the territory of the deceased Philip. Aretas was making a grab for Philip's tetrarchy and, apparently, its heavily Nabatean population preferred rule by Aretas to that of Antipas. In any case, the more important question about Aretas' territorial designs is whether he had a far grander scene in mind than mere control of the Hauran area.

The best explanation is that Aretas IV was—like Aretas III—making a thrust farther northward for Damascus itself. Aretas IV must have imagined ultimate Roman approval for a Nabatean Kingdom on a Petra-Damascus axis as a loyal desert buffer between the Roman and Parthian empires. Be that as it may, in late 36 CE, Aretas took control of Damascus and established an ethnarch there to protect Nabatean interests. Also, by holding Damascus, Aretas would control both the south-to-north and east-to-west desert trade routes that converged there.

Some such interpretation of Aretas IV's grand strategy is necessary to explain Tiberius' vehemently violent response. He ordered the new Syrian legate Vitellius "to declare war and either bring Aretas to him in chains . . . or send him his head" (*JA* 18.115). Aretas probably evacuated Damascus rather speedily but, in any case, Tiberius died in March 37, Vitellius abandoned his advance on Petra, and Aretas lived to die another day. That brings us back to Paul whose exit from Damascus was earlier but also rather precipitous:

> The God and Father of the Lord Jesus (blessed be he forever!) knows that I do not lie. In Damascus, the governor under King Aretas guarded the city of Damascus in order to seize me, but I was let down in a basket through a window in the wall, and escaped from his hands. (2 Cor 11:31–33)

As Aretas thrust northward, Paul probably moved to Damascus for safety but Aretas took control of that city in the winter of 36–37. That, by the way, gives us several relatively secure Pauline dates. He fled Damascus for Jerusalem in late 36 and dated that visit from his vocation-revelation as "after three years" (Gal 1:18). Hence Paul's vocation was in 33, his work in Arabia was from 33 to 36, and he made his first visit to Jerusalem in 36.

Luke, however, disagrees with both parts of Paul's immediate post-vocation account. First, instead of an Arabian Mission to Gentiles, there is—of course!—a Damascus Mission to Jews:

> For several days he was with the disciples in Damascus, and immediately he began to proclaim Jesus in the synagogues, saying, "He is the Son of God." . . . Saul became increasingly more powerful and confounded the Jews who lived in Damascus by proving that Jesus was the Messiah. (Acts 9:19b–22)

For Luke, as you recall, Paul is not the Apostle of the Gentiles but a great missionary who always goes, first, to his fellow Jews.

Next, for the escape, instead of Nabateans seeking to arrest Paul, Luke-Acts has Jews seeking to kill him:

> After some time had passed, the Jews plotted to kill him, but their plot became known to Saul. They were watching the gates day and night so that they might kill him; but his disciples took him by night and let him down through an opening in the wall, lowering him in a basket. (Acts 9:23–25)

Paul's Damascus escape is a classic proof that Luke-Acts has excellent Pauline geographical information but that he infused, refused, confused it with deliberate and programmatic theological (mis)interpretation for its own authorial intention and literary purpose. "The Jews" could never have guarded the gates of Damascus as potential killers and that makes Paul's exit under murderous Jewish threat as fictional as his arrival under high-priestly Jewish authority. And, as with his arrival, so with his departure from Damascus, Paul's own version is historically more credible and, besides, is autobiography given under oath. Read critically and judge carefully, therefore, what Luke-Acts says about murderous Jews—from Nazareth (Luke 4:29) to Damascus (Acts 9:23–24)—and elsewhere.

In any case, the result of Paul's return to and escape from Damascus (Gal 1:17=2 Cor 11:32–33) is that his Nabatean mission may have failed so completely that he never mentioned it other than in those rather short verses—and Luke-Acts omitted it completely.

Granted that Paul's first or Arabian Mission ended rather abruptly in that flight from Damascus, what about the preceding three years in the Hauran? If all had gone well there, why was there never a later Pauline *Letter to the Nabateans?* Or again, why did Paul not return there after Aretas IV's death in the year 40? Were there no Nabatean converts at all so that, in effect, the mission was a failure and its only success an escape? Also, did that create a theological problem for Paul's sense of his vocation-revelation? God sent him "among the Gentiles"; he went there immediately; but he failed dismally. To answer those questions, I do not attempt to read Paul's inner thoughts but to interpret his outer actions. What does he tell us he did next and, conversely, what does Luke-Acts say he did next?

————·····•••••••••••◇•••••••••••·····————

After his Damascus escape, Paul records two events: a visit to Jerusalem followed by departure to "Syria and Cilicia":

> Then after three years I did go up to Jerusalem to visit Cephas and stayed with him fifteen days; but I did not see any other apostle except James the Lord's brother. In what I am writing to you, before God, I do not lie! Then I went into the regions of Syria and Cilicia, and I was still unknown by sight to the churches of Judea that are in Christ. (Gal 1:18–22)

One note: Simon was bilingually nicknamed Cephas in Aramaic and Peter in Greek. Another note: Syria and Cilicia were temporarily combined into one Roman province in the 30s. Tacitus, for instance, speaks of "Syria Ciliciaque" at that time (*Annals* 6.31). So, in my best judgment, Paul left Jerusalem for Antioch on the Orontes, capital of the Roman province of Syria and Cilicia and not for the separated provinces of first Syria and then Cilicia.

As you expect by now, Luke's account is significantly different. Instead of an almost secret visit to Jerusalem where he was unknown to the community at large, Luke-Acts sends Paul back to a community which must have known him all too well since he was originally its highly authorized persecutor (Acts 26:9–11):

> When he had come to Jerusalem, he attempted to join the disciples; and they were all afraid of him, for they did not believe that he was a disciple. But Barnabas took him,

> brought him to the apostles, and described for them how
> on the road he had seen the Lord, who had spoken to
> him, and how in Damascus he had spoken boldly in the
> name of Jesus. So he went in and out among them in
> Jerusalem, speaking boldly in the name of the Lord. He
> spoke and argued with the Hellenists; but they were at-
> tempting to kill him. When the believers learned of it,
> they brought him down to Caesarea and sent him off to
> Tarsus. (9:26–30)

There are major Lukan-versus-Pauline contradictions within that
account—as happens regularly whenever we can compare Luke-
Acts and Paul on the same event.

First, Luke-Acts simply re-invents for Paul in Jerusalem what
he just invented for Paul in Damascus. At both locations, there were
doubts about the sincerity of Paul-the-convert and in both cases
Paul's confrontational witness to Jews results in a threat of death
from which he is rescued by "the disciples" who send him elsewhere—first from Damascus (9:19b–25) and then from Jerusalem
(9:26–30).

Next, Luke's account contradicts Paul's claim that he "was still
unknown by sight to the churches of Judea that are in Christ" (Gal
1:22). Indeed, as seen earlier, it even contradicts Luke's own claim
that Paul had started his public life as an officially accredited
super-persecutor in Jerusalem itself. Had he done so, his victims
would have known him by sight at least three years earlier!

Furthermore, Luke-Acts has Barnabas know immediately what
had happened in distant Damascus and know it precisely in Luke's own
version (9:1–6,19–22) which, as we have just seen, *fictionalizes* Paul's
sworn witness about what actually happened there (Gal 1:13–17).

Also, instead of Paul leaving from Jerusalem for "Syria and
Cilicia" (Gal 1:21), Luke-Acts has him leave from coastal Caesarea
for "Tarsus" (Acts 9:30). That is a Lukan misunderstanding of his
geographical information about Paul's departure to "Syria and Cilicia." Luke-Acts takes them as two separate Roman provinces and
thinks Paul went home to his native Tarsus (Acts 9:11; 21:39; 22:3)
probably, by the way, no longer a very welcoming location! Then,

later, granted that geographical misunderstanding, Luke-Acts says that "Barnabas went to Tarsus to look for Saul, and when he had found him, he brought him to Antioch" (Acts 11:25–26). But, one way or another, Barnabas and Paul eventually get together at Antioch. What, however, is the best historical reconstruction of what actually happened—especially assessing the Lukan claim that all important processes and persons start at and go forth from Jerusalem (Acts 1:8)?

First, Barnabas' contact with Paul is certainly not a passing invention of Luke-Acts which speaks about Barnabas repeatedly—from "Cyprus" in Acts 4:36 to "Cyprus" in 15:39. The pair are often cited in the surprising precedence of "Barnabas and Saul" (Acts 11:30; 12:25; 13:2,7) or "Barnabas and Paul" (Acts 14:14; 15:12,22). That indicates pre-Lukan traditions about Barnabas and Paul which agrees with Paul's own mention in that same name-order: "Barnabas and I" (1 Cor 9:6); "I . . . with Barnabas; . . . Barnabas and me . . . even Barnabas" (Gal 2:1,9,13).

Second, Barnabas' public life began when he came from his native Cyprus not to Jerusalem—against Acts 4:36—but directly to Antioch—from Acts 11:20. Thereafter: first, Barnabas and Paul are together in Jerusalem (9:27); next, they are together in Antioch (11:22,25); then, they are together in Jerusalem (11:30); and finally, they are together in Antioch (12:25; translate as: "returned, having finished their mission in Jerusalem" versus NRSV: "returned to Jerusalem"). That doubled Jerusalem-to-Antioch transition for both Barnabas-and-Paul asserts Luke's priority of Jerusalem for their first meeting but at least acknowledges Antioch as their eventual location.

Third, when Paul fled from Damascus to Jerusalem, he met secretly with Peter and James and then departed swiftly for Antioch after only "fifteen days" (Gal 1:18). But, for Paul, to go to Jerusalem was not to go "among the Gentiles." So why go there, why leave so swiftly, and why go to Antioch? Paul must have been somewhat lost between worlds both psychologically and theologically on that first Jerusalem visit. His divine mandate and apostolic status "among the Gentiles" had resulted, as I suggested earlier, in a three-year failure. My best guess is that the advice Paul received in Jerusalem was to leave—immediately—and connect with Barnabas at Antioch. In my opinion, James and Cephas hustled Paul out of Jerusalem swiftly for his and their own safety.

Finally, at Antioch, "for an entire year they [Barnabas and Paul] met with the church and taught a great many people, and it was in Antioch that the disciples were first called "Christians" (11:26). Why that? Why there? Why were the Messianic/Christics in Jerusalem not called "Christians"? Was it the Messianic/Christic Jews in Antioch who were called "Christians"? Or was it the Messianic/Christic Gentiles there who first got that name? If so, how and why did Paul have better success with the Gentiles of Syria than with those of Arabia? If Paul's vocation at Damascus was to go "among the Gentiles," did he have to undergo almost a second vocation-revelation at Antioch to specify precisely who were those "Gentiles" in terms of immediate missionary focus?

All of that leads to these questions for our next chapter: Who were those Antiochene converts called "Christians" and why was that new designation necessary—rather than, say, "Christian Jews"—on the analogy of Essene, Pharisaic, or Sadducean Jews? And, especially this: did and how did those "Christians" fit within Paul's divine mandate to go "among the Gentiles"? In answer, the next chapter begins rather far from Antioch in both time and place. It starts at Aphrodisias: a city dedicated to the Goddess Aphrodite; a city about 100 miles inland from the Aegean Sea; a city just off the Meander Valley on the western tip of the Anatolian Plateau; a city which Octavian, the not-yet Augustus, claimed as "the one city from all of Asia I have selected to be my own," because of his alleged descent from Aeneas, son of the Goddess Aphrodite and the Trojan shepherd Anchises.

Chapter 6

"YOU ISRAELITES, AND OTHERS WHO FEAR GOD, LISTEN"

Well, where is he [Paul] supposed to go? Where is he going to find people? In the Gentile agora? . . . He goes to the synagogue. . . . This is a spoken service; no sacrifices are brought here, hence also the attraction for many Greek and Roman intellectuals . . . whom others make fun of: that they go to the synagogues and even observe a day of rest. . . . In Greek they are called *sebomenoi*, the God-fearers. They were not Jews, but Gentiles . . . who went to the synagogue. . . . My thesis is that the Gentiles whom Paul made into Christians were originally recruited from . . . *sebomenoi* and that only later did other Gentiles join.

—Jacob Taubes, *The Political Theology of Paul*

After a 1960 earthquake, the tiny town of Geyre was relocated from atop the ruins of Greco-Roman Aphrodisias and excavations could begin there under Kenan Erim, a Turkish-born professor at New York University. He directed those still-on-going excavations until his death in 1990 and is buried on-site in the shadow of the main gate of Aphrodite's Temple. He once claimed that "of all the Graeco-Roman sites of Anatolia, Aphrodisias is the most hauntingly beautiful." It is precisely that. In it also for me, after ten visits there between 2000 and 2014, the most important archaeological site for understanding Roman Imperial Theology and also Pauline Messianic/Christic theology (Heresy: if you ever have to choose between Ephesus and Aphrodisias, head east!).

In 1976, during preparatory work for the new museum, a 9-foot-high marble column with four 18-inch-wide sides was discovered flat on the ground. Two of its three smoothed sides named donors and the fourth side was unsmoothed for positioning against a wall—presumably of the building financed by those inscribed on the first two sides. Almost everything about this column is controversial but for my present purpose I need primarily this factual datum. The two inscribed sides contain 125 names that include sixty-eight Jews (54.4 percent), three "converts" (2.4 percent), and fifty-four "God-worshipers" (43.2 percent). On one side, for example, Emmonios and Antōninos are termed *theoseb[ēs]*. On the other inscribed side, the title "And those who are God-worshipers" (*kai hosoi theosebis*) is followed by fifty-two names of which the first nine are specified as city "councillors" (*boul[eutēs]*). Please note and contemplate that percentage of "God-worshipers" who publicly proclaimed their financial support for some building presumably associated with the Aphrodisias synagogue.

Terms such as "God-worshipers" could, of course, be used for any very devout person—Jew or Gentile—in that first-century world. Josephus, for example, says that if his Egyptian antagonist Apion "were asked who, in his opinion, were the wisest and most God-fearing (*theosebeis*) of all the Egyptians," he would certainly name their polytheistic priests (*Against Apion* 2.140).

Still, especially in a context that connects them with the synagogue and contrasts them with native-Jews and "convert"-Jews, "God-worshipers" were not Gentile converts to Judaism but Gentile sympathizers with Judaism and Gentile supporters of Judaism. While remaining Gentiles—uncircumcised if male—they accepted the Jewish God, followed basic Jewish morality, observed the Jewish Sabbath by attendance at the local synagogue service, and were thereby well-versed in the Greek version of the Jewish scriptures.

That Aphrodisias column, dated most probably to the 300s–400s, does not indicate the belated arrival of a high percentage of such Gentile synagogue-supporters but rather the desire of those already there to make a very public manifesto directed polemically against ascendant post-Constantine Christianity. But it forces two questions from the fifth back to the first century. How many "God-fearers" were present among Jews in the Aphrodisias synagogue on any given sabbath in the 30s–40s CE? What were the comparative proportions of Jews to God-worshipers at any large urban synagogue that Paul would have visited in the first century CE?

For that first century, we also know of those Gentile Jewish-sympathizers from this reference to public synagogue education by Philo of Alexandria:

> On the seventh day there are spread before the people in every city innumerable lessons of prudence, and temperance, and courage, and justice, and all other virtues. . . . And there are, as we may say, two most especially important heads of all the innumerable particular lessons and doctrines; the regulating of one's conduct towards God by the rules of piety and holiness, and of one's conduct towards men by the rules of humanity and justice; each of which is subdivided into a great number of subordinate ideas, all praiseworthy. (*The Special Laws* 2.62–63)

Josephus agrees with that idyllic description from Philo but applies it more specifically to Syria in general and to Antioch—its inland capital on the Orontes River—in particular:

> The Jewish race, densely interspersed among the native populations of every portion of the world, is particularly numerous in Syria . . . due to the proximity of the two countries. But it was at Antioch that they specially congregated . . . grew in numbers . . . [and] they were constantly attracting to their religious ceremonies multitudes of Greeks, and these they had in some measure incorporated with themselves." (*JW* 7.43–45)

That phrase, "in some measure incorporated," shows the in-between position of God-worshipers between Antiochene Gentiles and Antiochene Jews. Furthermore, that status ambiguity became an acute problem in Syria at the start of the great Jewish revolt against Rome in 66–74:

> The whole of Syria was a scene of frightful disorder; every city was divided into two camps. . . [and the Gentiles] though believing they had rid themselves of the Jews,

> still each city had its Judaizers who aroused suspicion; and
> while they shrunk from killing offhand this equivocal ele-
> ment in their midst, they feared these neutrals as much as
> pronounced aliens. (*JW* 2.462–463)

Those equivocal and neutral Judaizers were recognizable, identifiable, and discoverable precisely as Gentile synagogue attendees and, as such, created a problem in the cruel warfare simplicity of Jews versus Gentiles.

About twenty years later, Josephus used a more specific term to distinguish between Jewish and non-Jewish donors to the Jerusalem Temple: "No one need wonder that there was so much wealth in our temple, for all the Jews throughout the habitable world, and those who worshipped God (*sebomenōn ton theon*), even those from Asia and Europe, had been contributing to it for a very long time" (*JA* 14.110). Notice both that precise Greek phrase and its explicit distinction from but association with "Jews"—to be seen again below in Luke-Acts.

Later in that same work, Josephus uses the compound term for a "God-worshiper." Around the year 60, the governor Porcius Festus allowed a high-level priestly delegation to appeal before Nero at Rome concerning some new construction overlooking Jerusalem's Temple. Nero agreed to their request: "In this he showed favor to his wife Poppaea, who was a God-worshiper (*theosebēs*) and who pleaded on behalf of the Jews" (*JA* 20.195)—that is, as you recall, the same Greek term used much later on the Aphrodisias column.

That Poppaea was a Gentile God-worshiper agrees with Josephus' personal experience of her a few years later. In 64, the new governor, Florus, sent certain priests "in bonds" to appear before Nero. When Josephus traveled to Rome for their defense, "I was introduced to Poppaea, Caesar's consort, and took the earliest opportunity of soliciting her aid to secure the liberation of the priests. Having besides this favor, received large gifts from Poppaea, I returned to my own country" (*Life 16*). Poppaea as a God-worshiper is probably how Nero knew to separate "Christians" from "Jews" as scapegoats for the Great Fire that same year of 64.

I presume that first-century God-worshiper matrix in turning now to answer the questions about Barnabas and especially about Barnabas-and-Paul from the end of the preceding chapter. My basic proposal is that Barnabas conducted a Gentile mission focused precisely on those God-worshipers in synagogues on the Sabbath at Antioch; that, after his failure in Arabia with unjudaized Gentiles, Paul went to Antioch and, following Barnabas' example, changed his understanding of "among the Gentiles" precisely to those judaized rather than unjudaized Gentiles—with and under Barnabas at Antioch; and that their mission to Cyprus was planned intentionally by Barnabas as an outreach from Antioch to his native Cyprus but focused on those Gentile synagogue-supporters already sympathetic to Judaism.

----·····◇······----

If I were to imagine an original title for Luke-Acts, it might be *The Way of the Holy Spirit* with *way* meaning both a route in geography and a life in theology. It is the Holy Spirit that commands and controls the Messianic/Christic drive from Jerusalem ever westward to Rome (Acts 19:21; 23:11). Hence, the mission of Barnabas-and-Paul across the northeastern Mediterranean heads westward for the island of Cyprus—under the command of the Holy Spirit:

> In the church at Antioch there were prophets and teachers: Barnabas, Simeon who was called Niger, Lucius of Cyrene, Manaen a member of the court of Herod the ruler, and Saul. While they were worshiping the Lord and fasting, the Holy Spirit said, "Set apart for me Barnabas and Saul for the work to which I have called them." Then after fasting and praying they laid their hands on them and sent them off. So, being sent out by the Holy Spirit, they went down to Seleucia; and from there they sailed to Cyprus. (Acts 13:1–4)

First, those sentences are the start of a new and independent Lukan source on Barnabas-and-Paul. That is why it reads as if we had not already heard much about Barnabas (4:36; 11:22,25), about Saul/Paul

(7:58; 8:1,3; 9:1–24), and about Barnabas-and-Saul/Paul (9:27; 11:30; 12:25). That source was probably a site-sequence accompanied by memorable incidents into which Luke—rhetorically trained to create speech-in-character and speech-in-context—could invent and insert speeches by Paul.

Second, after the mission had expanded beyond Cyprus to the Anatolian plateau and the southern half of Rome's Galatian province, Paul healed a lame man in the town of Lystra and, "When the crowds saw what Paul had done, they shouted in the Lycaonian language, 'The gods have come down to us in human form!' Barnabas they called Zeus, and Paul they called Hermes, because he was the chief speaker" (14:11–12). The sacrificial response from "the priest of Zeus" (14:13) is directed, of course, primarily to Barnabas as the leader.

Third, as you recall from Chapter 4, Luke-Acts negates Paul as an apostle sent directly by Christ and therefore equal to those earlier apostles in Jerusalem—apostle, as you know, is from Greek *apostellō*, to send. Luke, however, has no problem with calling Barnabas and Saul "apostles" sent on mission indirectly by the Holy Spirit but directly by that Antioch community. So safely and subordinately sent, they are called "apostles" several times on their mission (Acts 14:4,6,14).

—·····✦·····—

On landing at Salamis on the eastern coast of Cyprus, Barnabas and Paul "proclaimed the word of God in the synagogues of the Jews. And they had John also to assist them." Then, again without any Lukan details, they went "through the whole island as far as Paphos" (13:5–6), the capital of the Roman province of Cyprus and thus the seat of its proconsular governor.

At first glance, what follows in 13:6–12 seems a fabric(ation) woven of elements from elsewhere in Acts. The story contains a positive response from a proconsular-level Roman official—the first of three such reactions to Paul: from Sergius Paulus at Paphos, Gallio at Corinth (18:12–17), and Festus at Caesarea Maritima (26:31)—all part of Luke's Official Roman Exculpation theme. It also contains a successful contest against a magician—as with Peter against Simon in Samaria (14:18–24). It concludes with a punitive blindness that required being led "by the hand"—as with Paul himself into Damascus (9:8; 22:11).

Granted that, how is Acts 13:6–12 to be read critically—rather than just paraphrased uncritically or dismissed totally—within the authorial intention and apologetical themes of Luke-Acts? What in this story is factual Pauline information and what is fictional Lukan interpretation? In response, think about these four names in the story.

Elymas Bar-Jesus

At Paphos "they met a certain magician, a Jewish false prophet, named Bar-Jesus . . . the magician Elymas (for that is the translation of his name) opposed them" (13:6,8). Luke-Acts must have found the name "Elymas Bar-Jesus" in his Barnabas source and, not understanding it, supplied that rather desperate "translation" explanation. Recall, by the way, the exorcists at Ephesus who "tried to use the name of the Lord Jesus over those who had evil spirits, saying, 'I adjure you by the Jesus whom Paul proclaims'" and who were identified as "seven sons of the high priest Sceva"—presumably a Roman rather than a Jewish high priest (Acts 19:13–14). Elymas was a Jewish adviser who, although not a Messianic/Christic, operated through the invocation of the Jesus name and assumed the name Bar-Jesus.

Sergius Paulus

The governor of Cyprus, "the proconsul (*anthypatos*) Sergius Paulus" (13:7), was apparently superstitious and, from his viewpoint, found in Elymas versus Paul a contest between two opposing Jewish Bar-Jesus magicians. Barnabas and Paul—no doubt with far better information about this Jesus—must have prevailed.

Luke-Acts records this result at Paphos: "When the proconsul saw what had happened, he believed, for he was astonished at the teaching about the Lord" (13:12). Readers could easily conclude—as intended—that Saul had just converted a proconsul but, of course, Luke-Acts only claimed that Sergius Paulus "believed" Paul over Elymas and was "astonished at the teaching of the Lord" but not necessarily converted to live by it. Leaving aside Luke's prejudicial terms "magician" and "false prophet," the proconsul probably considered that it was all an entertaining contest between two philosopher-types.

Think, next, of the names on two broken inscriptions: one with "Quintus Ser[gius]," found on Cyprus and now in the Metropolitan Museum in New York; the other with "Paulli Ser[gii]" and L[ucius] Ser[gius] Paullus]," discovered near Pisidian Antioch, and now given pride of place inside the nearby Yalvaç Museum under a map of St. Paul's Travels and identified as "The St. Paul Inscription Stone." Those fragmentary references suggest that the familial home of Luke's Sergius Paulus was near Pisidian Antioch. If so, that might explain why a mission intended originally for Cyprus ended up on the Anatolian plateau. It may have been probably on the advice or maybe even under the patronage of the governor that Barnabas decided to take the mission to the governor's home territory at Pisidian Antioch.

John Mark

John Mark's first location was established and his importance emphasized in Jerusalem when Peter, having miraculously escaped prison, "went to the house of Mary, the mother of John whose other name was Mark, where many had gathered and were praying" (Acts 12:12). Later, "after completing their mission at (*eis*) Jerusalem, Barnabas and Saul returned [to Antioch] and brought with them John, whose other name was Mark" (Acts 12:25, retranslated!).

Next, there is that just-seen mention of John's assistance on Cyprus (Acts 13:5) but, later, when "Paul and his companions set sail from Paphos and came to Perga in Pamphylia. John, however, left them and returned to Jerusalem" (Acts 13:13)—not to Antioch, note, but to Jerusalem. John-Mark stayed and left but why was that worth mentioning?

Here is how I reconstruct the significance of John-Mark of Jerusalem. First, I think he was sent by the Jerusalem authorities to accompany and report about this programmatic mission among the Gentiles and how it would handle Jews versus Gentiles in common situations. Presumably, therefore, the mission was originally approved by Jerusalem only for Cyprus and that is why John-Mark refused to go any farther (Acts 13:13). In any case, note this later and final mention of John-Mark:

> After some days Paul said to Barnabas, "Come, let us return and visit the believers in every city where we proclaimed the word of the Lord and see how they are doing." Barnabas wanted to take with them John called Mark. The disagreement became so sharp that they parted company; Barnabas took Mark with him and sailed away to Cyprus. (Acts 15:36–39)

As we shall see below, it was Barnabas' acceptance of Jerusalem's missionary oversight that forced Paul eventually to break with him (Galatians 2:13=Acts 15:39) and my guess is that a dispute had started already between Barnabas and Paul about John-Mark on the Cypro-Anatolian Mission. Luke-Acts makes that all seem a minor matter of personality, character, and convenience rather than a major one of authority, jurisdiction, and control.

Saul Paul

Two questions arise concerning Luke-Acts' claim about "Saul, also known as Paul" (13:9). First, did he have two names, Saul-Paul, which, despite any similarity, have nothing to do with one another linguistically? That double name is quite possible and, in itself, hardly worth much debate. But Paul himself never mentions it even when, asserting his natal Jewishness, he notes that he was of "the tribe of Benjamin" (Phil 3:5; Rom 11:1) whose most famous son was Saul (1 Sam 9:1–2). That double name, then, is possible, but unlikely.

Much more significant is this second question. Whether that double name is factual or fictional, why did Luke-Acts always use "Saul" up to that pivot point in Acts 13:9 and always use "Paul" thereafter—except on the lips of Christ at Damascus (9:4; 22:7; 26:14)?

It was only after Sergios Paulos was named (13:7) that Saul was renamed Paulos (13:9) and, within Luke-Acts' Romanization of the Messianic/Christic tradition, that timing is suspiciously tendentious. The implication of that name change in that location at that moment was that Sergius Paulus became a sponsor for Saul who, as a respectful client, assumed his patron's family name Paul. This is, for Luke-Acts, the symbolic moment when the Jewish Saul becomes the Roman Paul. All in all, therefore, and whatever about a double name *Saul-and-Paul*, that absolute transition from *Saul-to-Paul* after Sergius Paulus at Paphos is a Lukan pro-Roman apologetical fiction.

----·····━━━━━━✦━━━━━━·····─

Although Luke-Acts mentioned that the missionaries "proclaimed the word of God in the synagogues of the Jews" (13:5) on Cyprus, we got no details of what happened in those places. The obvious presumption is that they went to those synagogues to convert Jews, that is to make them into Messianic/Christic Jews. But, if so, how could Paul have ever agreed to participate in such a program? His divine revelation, vocation, and mandate was "to proclaim him [God's Son] among the Gentiles" (Gal 1:16)—not among the Jews.

There is no explicit answer to that question in Luke-Acts material on Cyprus but there might be an implicit one. I think Luke-Acts wants readers to consider Sergius Paulus as almost a Gentile sympathizer and as something like a God-worshiper. He is a quasi-continuation of the "God-fearers" at Caesarea (10:2,22,35) and a quasi-preparation for the transition from "God-fearers" (13:16,26) to "God-worshipers" (13:43,50) at—and after—Pisidian Antioch (16:14; 17:4,17; 18:7). Be that as it may, the answer gets explicitly clear once Barnabas and Paul reach the Anatolian plateau.

From Pamphylian Perga on the coast (Acts 13:13) they took the longer but safer Roman Via Sebaste—built under Augustus in 6 BCE—which curved westward around the Pisidian Lakes up into the Phrygian highlands—with Pisidian Antioch as its road-head (13:14). From that colony (*colonia*) of legionary veterans they continued on the same roadway through Iconium (13:51) to another colony of legionary veterans at Lystra (14:6) and then on to Derbe (14:6,20) although that was probably by a side road. But watch first what happened at Pisidian Antioch.

First, the double audience. Recall, from earlier in this book, how Luke's parallelism of Peter-and-Paul created a pattern of Peter-over-Paul and how that process was emphasized by the triple invocation of audience in each's inaugural speech to fellow-Jews. Peter's speech at Jerusalem was directed to his fellow-Jews: "Men of Judea and all who live in Jerusalem . . . You that are Israelites . . . Fellow Israelites." (2:14,22,29). But Paul's corresponding speech at Pisidian Antioch had a double audience of both Jewish synagogue members and Gentile synagogue-supporters: "You Israelites, and others who fear God (*phoboumenoi ton theon*) . . . My brothers, you descendants of Abraham's family, and others who fear God (*phoboumenoi ton theon*) . . . my brothers." (13:16,26,38)

Second, the pattern of response. Luke-Acts had inaugurally established a fourfold sequence concerning Jew-and-Gentile with his story about Jesus at Nazareth. There, he had very deliberately changed his Markan source by turning Jesus' first Sabbath of complete triumph in Capernaum's synagogue (Mark 1:21–28) into a first Sabbath of lethal disaster in Nazareth's synagogue (Luke 4:16–30). Here is Luke's four-point pattern at Nazareth:

First, the proclamation of Jesus as Messiah (4:16–21)
Next, the initial Jewish reaction is positive (4:22)
Then, the Gentile participation is mentioned (4:23–27)
Finally, the initial Jewish response turns lethal (4:28–30).

I do not think that ever happened at Nazareth or that Jesus' fellow villagers were murderous "Jews." That is a Lukan fiction projecting later opposition to Paul inaugurally back onto Jesus. But that fiction is also a major indication that Luke-Acts was conceived and composed, produced and published as a single two-volume work *ab initio*. Luke-Acts was already preparing for Paul as it was writing about Jesus. That fourfold Nazareth pattern now reappears with Paul at Pisidian Antioch but with much more historical plausibility for negative reactions to the poaching of Gentile supporters in Sabbath-synagogue situation:

First, the proclamation of Jesus as Messiah: "They . . .
came to Antioch in Pisidia. And on the sabbath day they
went into the synagogue and sat down. . . . 'God has brought
to Israel a Savior Jesus, as . . . promised.'" (13:14,23)

Next, the initial Jewish reaction is positive: "When the
meeting of the synagogue broke up, many Jews and devout converts to Judaism (*sebomenōn prosēlytōn*) followed
Paul and Barnabas, who spoke to them and urged them
to continue in the grace of God." (13:42–43)

Then, the Gentile participation is mentioned: "The
next sabbath almost the whole city gathered to hear the
word of the Lord. But when the Jews saw the crowds,
they were filled with jealousy; and blaspheming, they contradicted what was spoken by Paul." (13:44–45)

Finally, the initial Jewish response turns lethal: "The
Jews incited the devout women of high standing and the
leading men of the city, and stirred up persecution against
Paul and Barnabas, and drove them out of their region.
So they shook the dust off their feet in protest against
them, and went to Iconium." (13:50–51)

Ignore Luke's mistaken term "converts" since, as we know from the
start of this chapter, those "God-fearers" or "God-worshipers" are
not converts to Judaism but sympathizers with Judaism as indicated
publicly by supporting and attending Sabbath-synagogue services.

My proposal—from Luke-Acts but against Luke-Acts—is that
Barnabas-and-Paul did not go to Sabbath synagogues to convert
Jews and just happen to find and attract Gentile supporters there.
Instead their mission strategy was to go to Sabbath synagogues be-
cause where else would they find and how else could they recognize
such Gentile God-fearers/worshipers? They went to those Sabbath
synagogues not to persuade their Jewish members but to poach their
Gentile sympathizers.

Furthermore, such deliberate and successful poaching of Gentile God-fearers/worshipers in Sabbath synagogues would necessarily have led to Jews versus Jews, Gentile supporters versus Gentile
supporters, and widening civil unrest and urban turmoil. No wonder,

therefore, that, as they moved along the Via Sebaste, what happened at Pisidian Antioch was repeated at Iconium and again at Lystra:

> At Iconium: "a great number of both Jews and Greeks became believers. But the unbelieving Jews stirred up the Gentiles and poisoned their minds against the brothers. . . . The residents of the city were divided; some sided with the Jews, and some with the apostles. . . . An attempt was made by both Gentiles and Jews, with their rulers, to mistreat them and to stone them." (14:1–5)
>
> At Lystra: "Jews came there from Antioch and Iconium and won over the crowds. Then they stoned Paul and dragged him out of the city, supposing that he was dead. But when the disciples surrounded him, he got up and went into the city." (14:19–20a)

That poaching of Gentiles in the synagogue on the Sabbath was, of course, rather different from preaching to Gentiles in the Forum on a Festival. When, according to Luke, Paul tried that latter mission strategy at Athens, "in the marketplace every day with those who happened to be there," the result among pure Gentiles was not lethal attack but mocking dismissal (17:17–32).

One question—maybe even an objection. Paul speaks regularly of "Jews and Gentiles" (Gal 2:14; 1 Cor 1:23) or, more often, of "Jews and Greeks" (Gal 3:28; 1 Cor 10:32; 12:13; Rom 1:16; 2:9–10; 3:19; 10:12), but he never mentions his Gentiles or Greeks as "God-fearers" or "God-worshipers."

Luke-Acts, however, and it alone in the entire New Testament, repeatedly mentions those pro-Jewish Gentile synagogue-supporters and names them as: "God-fearers" (*phoboumenoi ton theon*) in Acts 10:2, 22, 35; 13:16, 26); "God-worshipers" (*sebomenoi ton theon*) in Acts 16:14; 18:7; or simply "worshipers" (*sebomenoi*) in Acts 13:43, 50; 17:4, 17, which the NRSV translates as "devout"). Why is Luke-Acts so interested in them?

My answer is that the author of Luke-Acts was a God-fearer/worshiper and wrote especially for those who were now, like its unknown author, Messianic/Christic God-fearers or God-worshipers.

That would explain why this author knows the Jewish biblical tradition so well and yet is so severely prejudiced against Jews—recall that bias in Luke 4:29 and Acts 9:23–24.

It would also explain why John 4:46–53 and Q in Matt 8:5-13=the Lukan 7:1-10 tell the story of that Capernaum official but only Luke-Acts adds in that, "he sent some Jewish elders to him, asking him [Jesus] to come and heal his slave. When they came to Jesus, they appealed to him earnestly, saying, 'He is worthy of having you do this for him, for he loves our people, and it is he who built our synagogue for us'" (Luke 7:3–5). That official is, for Luke-Acts, a synagogue supporter, that is implicitly a God-fearer/worshiper who turns to Jesus.

Finally, Luke-Acts dedicates both his volumes to "Theophilus" (*Theophile* in Luke 1:3; Acts 1:1). Whether that is a specific individual or a personified group, I take "God-lover" as another Lukan term for "God-fearer/worshiper." Luke-Acts writes to reassure them not about their religious security under God but about their political safety under Rome (hence *asphaleia* in Luke 1:4 is not about theological "truth" and accuracy but about social "safety" and security).

After the shock of failure with unjudaized Gentiles in Arabia, Paul—now under Barnabas' leadership—accepted his apostolic mission "among the Gentiles" as primarily focused among judaized Gentiles, among those God-fearers/worshipers to be found in synagogues on the Sabbath. They became for Paul his divinely mandated "Gentiles."

Chapter 7

"WE SHOULD GO TO THE GENTILES AND THEY TO THE CIRCUMCISED"

We know of the Jerusalem conference's existence and stakes only through Paul's own brief narrative, and through its staging in the Acts. That it ended in compromise, in a sort of delimitation of spheres of influence, is certain. . . . Peter is apostle of the Jews; Paul, apostle of the Gentiles. . . . Everything, including Paul's defensive tone . . . shows that the compromise was unstable, which is not to say it was without historical influence.

—Alain Badiou, *Saint Paul: The Foundation of Universalism*

In antiquity, the Levantine coast of the Mediterranean was the hinge between the three continents of Europe, Asia, and Africa and also, not surprisingly, the avenue of empire. Israel was thus a cockpit for paired superpower aggression; first, it was north against south, with Mesopotamia against Egypt; next, it was west against east, with Greeks against Persians, and Romans against Parthians. Or, more locally, between 270 and 170 BCE, there were six wars between Egypt and Syria—with Israel in between as a useful battleground. The promised land might have flowed with yogurt and honey but it also flowed with destruction and devastation. From that came two rather extraordinary—and almost contradictory—reactions and results.

One result was that tiny Israel managed to survive as a people in that most dangerous location when other ethnic groups disappeared into the melting pot and gene pool of the Middle East. On the one hand, they survived by communal faith in a God who had given them their land in a covenant invoking fidelity to distributive socio-economic justice and loyalty to a protective ethnico-cultural screen built around it. On the other hand, they solved the cognitive

dissonance between faith in a just Creator and experience of an unjust Creation by dreaming of "days to come" when God would clean
up the cosmic mess of an unjust world.

At that great moment, to the background beat of an anvil chorus turning swords into plowshares and spears into pruning hooks
(Isa 2:2–4; Mic 4:1–4), the nations would stream to Jerusalem for a
magnificent cosmic feast celebrating universal peace (Isa 25:6–8). But
Isaiah never asked these two questions: when those Gentiles travel
to join the Jews, will their males be circumcised in transit; and will
the menu for that great feast be kosher for all or kosher for none?
Furthermore, when that great day dawned, would God's cosmic deliverance require angelic or human leadership and, if human, would
that Appointed Leader, that Anointed One, that Messiah/Christ, be
of royal, prophetic, priestly—or other—lineage?

Eventually, however, by the first century CE, against the backdrop
of Gentiles streaming to Jerusalem but specifically as conquering
legions, those future prophetic promises became present practical
problems. Think of them as a tri-level challenge for both Jewish homeland and Jewish diaspora.

The first challenge was whether Jesus of Nazareth was the
Messiah/Christ and, if yes, then had the Messianic/Christic Age
arrived not as an end-time divine intervention but as an in-time
divine and human cooperation?

The second challenge—for those who said yes to that preceding one—was whether those Gentile males prophesied to enter
God's people in the Messianic/Christic Age would have first to be
circumcised.

The third challenge—for those who answered yes to that preceding twosome—was whether common meals for Messianic/Christic
Jews and Messianic/Christic Gentiles should be kosher for both or
kosher for neither.

One caution before continuing. If you find those ancient
disputes over circumcision and kosher obsoletely irrelevant today,
imagine how our divisions over race and gender may appear—if our
species still survives—two millennia from now. Beneath all such divides—then, now, always—is the correct conservative claim that if you

change it, you might lose it, against the correct liberal counter-claim that if you do not change it, you will lose it. Evolution is change and, since we do not like change, we ignore evolution—which makes us contented, complacent, and doomed.

Watch, next, how those latter two challenges from that above triad were negotiated among inaugural groups who had already responded affirmatively to the first one by proclaiming Jesus as their Messiah/Christ.

Whether you call it the Jerusalem Conference or Council, Debate or Dispute, that event is certainly the same one described by both Paul (Gal 2:1–10) and Luke-Acts (15:1–35). But, once again, the differences between Paul and Luke-Acts are as significant as those already seen so far concerning just about everything important.

First, the Subject. The main subject of the meeting was the question of circumcision for male converts to the Messianic/Christic community. Here is Luke's account of how that question was raised:

> Certain individuals came down from Judea and were teaching the brothers, "Unless you are circumcised according to the custom of Moses, you cannot be saved." And after Paul and Barnabas had no small dissension and debate with them, Paul and Barnabas and some of the others were appointed to go up to Jerusalem to discuss this question with the apostles and the elders. (Acts 15:1–2)

Paul agrees that male-convert circumcision was at least the subject of the visit: "Titus, who was with me, was not compelled to be circumcised, though he was a Greek" (Gal 2:1,3).

Second, the Participants. For Luke-Acts, the meeting involved the "apostles and the elders" (15:2,6,23) but also "the church . . . the whole assembly . . . the consent of the whole church" (15:4,12,22).

For Paul, his first visit to Jerusalem was private, if not secret—he saw only Peter and James (Gal 1:18–19). This second one was as private even if not as secret as that former one (Gal 2:2).

On this second visit there are three protagonists on each side: Barnabas, Paul, and Titus versus James, Peter, and John.[1] The debate was held "only in a private meeting with those who were the acknowledged leaders" (Gal 2:2). It was not, *pace* Luke-Acts, a communal meeting of the entire assembly, congregation, or church.

Third, the Rhetoric. Focus, to start with, on how Paul sums up the outcome of the dispute: "from those who were supposed to be acknowledged leaders (what they actually were makes no difference to me; God shows no partiality)—those leaders contributed nothing to me" (Gal 2:6). The polite but inadequate NRSV translation calls those Jerusalem authorities "those who were supposed to be acknowledged leaders" and "leaders" but the dismissive Greek term is *hoi dokountes*, that is, the "seeming ones." (Greek has a perfectly good word for "leaders" in *hēgoumenoi*—as in Acts 15:22—but it is a word Paul never uses anywhere). In fact, within only eight verses, Paul cites James, Simon-Peter-Cephas, and John three times as *hoi dokountes* or "seeming ones" and then finally once as *hoi dokountes styloi* or "seeming pillars" (2:2,6ab,9).

The King James Bible struck precisely the right note when it translated Gal 2:6 with a doubled "those who seemed to be something." The properly dismissive translation is: "seeming somebodies" or "seeming ones" or "so-called ones" or "alleged ones" or any type of "ones" but certainly not "acknowledged leaders" (as in the NRSV). All of that is, from Paul, a rather heavy dose of rhetorical

---

[1] *On James.* This is James the Just, James of Jerusalem, "James the Lord's brother" (Gal 1:19), "James, the brother of Jesus who was called the Christ" (Josephus, *JA* 2.200); and also "James, a servant of God and of the Lord Jesus Christ," the fictional author of that eponymous epistle (James 1:1).

On Cephas. Simon had a bilingual nickname: Cephas in Aramaic, Petros in Greek (and Rocky in English). "'You are Simon son of John. You are to be called Cephas' (which is translated Peter)" said Jesus (John 1:42).

On John. This is John of "James and John," the sons of Zebedee (Mark passim); John of "Peter and John" (Acts passim); James had been executed in Acts 12:2.

contempt—especially for those who were at least ultimately in agreement with his position on no circumcision for Messianic/Christic male converts.

Finally, the Decision. The final decree favored Paul's position on no circumcision for male Messianic/Christic converts and Paul cites it in triplicate:

> When they saw that I had been entrusted with the gospel for the uncircumcised, just as Peter had been entrusted with the gospel for the circumcised
>
> (for he who worked through Peter making him an apostle to the circumcised also worked through me in sending me to the Gentiles),
>
> when James and Cephas and John, who were acknowledged pillars, recognized the grace that had been given to me, they gave to Barnabas and me the right hand of fellowship, agreeing that we should go to the Gentiles and they to the circumcised. (Gal 2:7–9)

But no matter how often Paul repeated that decision, it was a fundamental administrative compromise, a fateful act of missionary separation, an unworkable division between groups living in the same cities and attending the same synagogues as Jewish members or Gentile supporters. (It is as if Roman Catholicism finally accepted female alongside male priests—but with male ones only for men and female ones only for women.) Needless to say, there is not the slightest hint of any such compromise solution or mission separation in Luke-Acts' account of the—for it—beautifully collegial and magnificently irenic Jerusalem Conference (Acts 15:1–29).

———————◇———————

At the start of this chapter, we noted three inaugural challenges arising from the Messianic/Christic vision in the early first century. That just-seen executive meeting in Jerusalem "solved" the second challenge—about circumcision for male Gentile converts (Gal 2:1–10). But that also made the third one inevitable—about common meals for Gentile and Jewish converts. That challenge too arose on the fault line between Jerusalem's conservative authority and Antioch's liberal creativity. And, once again, Paul's rhetoric was bitter and biting but now also much more pointed and personal (Gal 2:11–14).

The back-story of this third challenge is that—as agreed at Jerusalem—Peter and Paul were conducting their separate mission at Antioch and "until certain people came from James, he [Peter] used to eat with the Gentiles. But after they came, he drew back and kept himself separate for fear of the circumcision faction" (2:12). Peter and Paul had agreed to hold common meals for Messianic/Christic Jews and Messianic/Christic Gentiles on a kosher-for-none basis. James of Jerusalem insisted instead on common meals with a kosher-for-all menu.

Paul accused Peter of "hypocrisy" for that flip-flop: "I opposed him to his face, because he stood self-condemned. . . . I said to Cephas before them all, 'If you, though a Jew, live like a Gentile and not like a Jew, how can you compel the Gentiles to live like Jews?'" (2:11, 14). In other words, how can you, who once practiced kosher-for-none, turn now to kosher-for-all—in common meals for Messianic/Christic Jews and Messianic/Christic Gentiles?

Furthermore, "the other Jews joined him in this hypocrisy, so that even Barnabas was led astray by their hypocrisy" (2:13). Notice, by the way, that "the circumcision faction" is alive and well even after or especially after that Jerusalem decision. Paul was left alone—and angrily alone—in his accusatory dissent. What happened after that bitter dispute at Antioch?

Luke-Acts admits that there was a missionary separation between Barnabas and Paul at Antioch. He even calls it a "sharp disagreement" but claims that the issue was about taking John Mark with them despite his refusal to go beyond Cyprus on the earlier Cypro-Anatolian Mission (13:13). The result, according to Luke-Acts, was that the earlier Cypro-Anatolian Mission was repeated but now split into two parts: Barnabas and Mark "sailed away to Cyprus," with John Mark once again as Jerusalem's authoritative presence (15:39); Paul and Silas returned to the Anatolian cities of southern Galatia—Iconium, Lystra, and Derbe (15:40–16:5).

—··········⟨◇⟩·········——

One footnote or postscript to that Antioch fracas over kosher for-all or kosher-for-none in common meals for Messianic/Christic Jews and Gentiles. It is fascinating, for example, to compare Paul's earlier response to the challenge of such meals at Antioch (Gal 2:11–14) with his later one on such meals at Rome (Rom 14:1–15:1). For Antioch, he immediately and vehemently rejected kosher-for-all but, for Rome, he serenely defended and accepted it. We have just seen that former case, here is the latter one.

First, Paul announces his principle on kosher rules: "I know and am persuaded in the Lord Jesus that nothing is unclean in itself; but it is unclean for anyone who thinks it unclean" (14:1). But, even if "everything is indeed clean, . . . it is wrong for you to make others fall by what you eat" (14:20).

Next, rather condescendingly, Paul distinguishes in the Messianic/Christic community between "those who are weak in faith" and retain kosher rules (14:1) and "we who are strong" and reject them (15:1). But, on this subject of "eating" (14:2,3,6,15,20,21,23), "those who eat must not despise those who abstain, and those who abstain must not pass judgment on those who eat" (14:3).

Finally, despite that mutuality, Paul's admonitions speak more to the strong than to the weak: "If your brother or sister is being injured by what you eat, you are no longer walking in love. Do not let what you eat cause the ruin of one for whom Christ died" (14:15). Again: "the kingdom of God is not food and drink but righteousness and peace and joy in the Holy Spirit" (14:17). Therefore, confronted with a situation of kosher commensality, "We who are strong ought to put up with the failings of the weak, and not to please ourselves" (15:1).

What if, confronted with James, Peter, and Barnabas at Antioch, Paul had used that admittedly most condescending argument—at least internally to himself—in favor of kosher-for-all in common meals? Or was that third or commensality problem an immediate indication that the two-mission solution to the circumcision problem was a doomed compromise from the very start?

In any case, those crises at Jerusalem and Antioch were intensely personal for Paul because they threatened both his divine vocation among the Gentiles and his equal standing among the apostles—those who were simply "already apostles before me" (Gal 1:17) or with whom he was "the least of the apostles, unfit to be called an apostle, because I persecuted the church of God" (1 Cor 15:9). Still, as you will see next, there was an earlier crisis for Paul in Galatia itself that was more bodily and existentially personal than even those later vocational and professional crises at Jerusalem, at Antioch, or in the bitter invective of the letter to the Galatians.

———·····:·:::=:::+=+◇=+::::·:::.····———

Paul had met the Galatians only as a second-in-command to Barnabas and, because of that subordination, they seem not to have known the story of his Damascus vocation. When he introduces it, the translation, "I want you to know" about it (Gal 1:11) is stronger in the Greek original, something like: "I make known to you (*gnōrizō gar hymin*)," as if they were hearing this for the first time. Be that as it may, he later makes this plaintively nostalgic and physically personal admission about their initial relationship:

> You know that it was because of a physical infirmity (*di' asthenian tēs sarkos*) that I first announced the gospel to you; though my condition put you to the test, you did not scorn or despise me, but welcomed me as an angel of God, as Christ Jesus. What has become of the good will you felt? For I testify that, had it been possible, you would have torn out your eyes and given them to me. (4:13–15)

Notice the force of that "first announced" and its inference that without some "physical infirmity" Paul might not have proclaimed the gospel "to you." Also, watch that surprising counterpoint between Paul's debilitated physical status and their acceptance of him as almost a divine presence. Furthermore, it looks like that "physical infirmity" effected his eyes in some way. Finally, any explanation must keep in mind this next Pauline text.

Paul was once forced against his better judgment into a bragging competition with those he derisively called "super-apostles" at Corinth (2 Cor 11:5; 12:11). But, while admittedly boasting like a "fool," he will only identify himself obliquely by saying that, "I know a person in Christ who fourteen years ago . . . was caught up into Paradise and heard things that are not to be told, that no mortal is permitted to repeat" (2 Cor 12:2–3). He repeats twice that his ecstatic experience was "in the body or out of the body I do not know; God knows" (12:2,3). Then comes this very famous line: "considering the exceptional character of the revelations . . . to keep me from being too elated, a thorn was given me in the flesh (*skolops tēi sarki*), a messenger of Satan to torment me, to keep me from being too elated" (12:7). That word "thorn" is, by the way, much too weak a translation of the Greek word *skolops* which means a stake.

With many other scholars, I presume that Paul's "thorn in the flesh" was some chronic disease of which the Galatian "physical infirmity" was but one recurrence. For example, Joseph Barber Lightfoot[2], English theologian and later Bishop of Durham, connected them together with the thorn, "a return of his old malady . . . some sharp and violent attack . . . which humiliated him and prostrated his physical strength" (page 29). But what was that "old malady" and how does it fit with the details in both those Pauline texts?

My answer adopts gratefully but adapts critically the solution proposed over a century-and-a-quarter ago by (later Sir) William Mitchell Ramsay, Professor of Latin Humanity at the University of Aberdeen in Scotland from 1886 to 1911. I especially respect that solution for his earlier travel experiences around the Pauline sites under discussion. Ramsay made three points on Paul's disease. For the first one, recall that "Paul and his companions set sail from Paphos and came to Perga in Pamphylia" (Acts 13:13). But, according to Ramsay:[3]

---

[2] Joseph Barber Lightfoot, *St. Paul's Epistle to the Galatians*. A Revised Text. Andover MA: Warren Fales Draper, 1870. Read online from the Internet Archive.

[3] William Ramsay, *The Church in the Roman Empire before A.D. 170*. London, UK: Hodder & Stoughton, 1893. Based on his Mansfield College Lectures at Oxford University in 1892. Read online from the Internet Archive.

Every one who has travelled in Pamphylia knows how relaxing and enervating the climate is. In these low-lying plains fever is endemic; the land is so moist as to be extraordinarily fertile and the most dangerous to strangers. Confined by the vast ridges of Taurus, 5,000 to 9,000 feet high, the atmosphere is like the steam of a kettle, hot, moist, and swept by no north winds. . . . We suppose then that Paul caught fever on reaching Perga in Pamphylia. (pages 62–63)

Ramsay continues by specifying Paul's fever as "malarial fever" (typical symptoms would have been high fever, chills, sweating, muscle pain, headache, blurring of vision, and dizziness.) He also suggests that it was, "precisely after fatigue and hardship, travelling on foot through Cyprus amid great excitement and mental strain, that one was peculiarly liable to be affected by the sudden plunge into the enervating atmosphere of Pamphylia" (page 63).

Then, in order to contrast the climate of Cyprus, swept by sea breezes, with that of Pamphylia, squeezed between sea and mountain, Ramsay records this anecdote:

In August 1890 I met on the Cilician coast an English officer on his way home from three years' duty in Cyprus: previously he had spent some years in Eastern service. He said that the climate of the Cilician coast (which is very similar to that of Pamphylia, and has not any worse reputation for unhealthiness) reminded him of Singapore or Hong Kong, while that of Cyprus was infinitely fresher and more invigorating." (page 63)

Despite citing Lightfoot's "return of his old malady" (page 63); despite comparing the unhealthy climate of the Cilician and Pamphylian plains; despite knowing that Tarsus, capital of Cilicia, was the birthplace of Paul according to Acts 22:3, Ramsay never makes the seemingly obvious conclusion that Paul's thorn/stake was chronic malarial fever from his natal Tarsus that reoccurred at—for Ramsay—Perga.

Second, Ramsay[4] returned, defensively, to that interpretation in a later book by speaking of a "latent weakness of constitution . . . the same malady which tormented him at frequent intervals . . . this malady was a species of chronic malarial fever" (page 54). But, that "chronic malarial fever" is negated by his conclusion that, "the malady certainly did not begin long before this journey; and the attack in Pamphylia may perhaps have been the first" (page 56).

Finally, Ramsay[5] wrote:

> In respect of the danger of malaria the case of Tarsus was similar to that of Perga, and even worse. Perga stood on a slightly elevated plateau by the river: Tarsus lay on the dead level plain, only a few feet above the lowest level of the river Cydnus, and exposed to inundation as soon as the water rose in flood. (page 96)

But he still does not draw the more obvious conclusion that it was Paul's chronic malarial malady from Tarsus that reoccurred—for Ramsay—at Perga. So, what conclusions should be drawn from all of that data?

I take two major elements from Lightfoot and Ramsay. First, Paul's "thorn/stake in the flesh" was chronic malaria and that his "physical infirmity" in Galatia was a typical reoccurrence of it. Second, the reoccurrence of such a chronic illness was usually brought on by some immediately preceding cause that left the sufferer in a severely debilitated and extremely weakened condition. But I make two major adaptations to that explanation because, bluntly, Pauline malaria at Perga is a non-starter (pun intended).

---

[4] William Mitchell Ramsay, *St. Paul the Traveler and the Roman Citizen.* Tenth edition. London UK: Hodder & Stoughton, 1907. Read online from Christian Classics Ethereal Library.

[5] William Mitchell Ramsay, *The Cities of Saint Paul: Their influence on His Life and Thought* (The Cities of Eastern Asia Minor). New York, NY: Hodder & Stoughton/George H. Doran Company, 1907. Based on the Dale Memorial lectures at Mansfield College of Oxford University, 1907. Read online from the Internet Archive.

First, a malarial attack at Perga that was still fully there by at least Pisidian Antioch meant that, in his fevered state, Paul had slogged 150 miles on the Via Sebaste—a trip calculated to deliver him upland in a coffin rather than in the full paroxysm of malarial fever. How, then, how was Paul's mission in Galatia plausibly due to a recurrent attack of chronic malarial fever, where did the attack occur, and why was it caused there?

As we saw already, Luke-Acts records lethal persecution for Barnabas and Paul at Iconium where "an attempt was made by both Gentiles and Jews, with their rulers, to mistreat them and to stone them" (14:5). That opposition came to climax at Lystra when,

> Jews came there from Antioch and Iconium and won over the crowds. Then they stoned Paul and dragged him out of the city, supposing that he was dead. But when the disciples surrounded him, he got up and went into the city. The next day he went on with Barnabas to Derbe. (14:19–20)

Paul, by the way, agrees that "once I received a stoning" (2 Cor 11:25). Then, even after such an almost-fatal experience, Luke-Acts continues almost casually with this account of what happened at Derbe: "After they had proclaimed the good news to that city and had made many disciples, they returned to Lystra, then on to Iconium and Antioch" (14:21). For the record, after what had happened at Antioch, Iconium, and Lystra, I doubt that the mission immediately reversed course through those inimical locations. Instead it probably continued overland home to Syrian Antioch.

In any case, and however the Cypro-Anatolian Mission returned home, Derbe is the best location for Paul's "physical infirmity" and it was apparently not on the mission's original travel plan. The only reason they ended up there was for refuge and safety from and after Antioch, Iconium, and Lystra.

After the terror of a stoning and the strain of a three-day flight from Lystra to Derbe, Paul suffered at Derbe a full attack of his chronic malarial malady. That situation meant that they "welcomed me as an angel of God, as Christ Jesus"—which responded to a Paul semi-martyred by stoning—and "did not scorn or despise me"— which responded to a Paul semi-obliterated by malaria.

Still, if Paul was stricken with malarial fever only in Derbe how can his letter speak of it as if it were the cause of the entire Galatian mission? As a circular letter to those various south Galatian cities he had visited, "You know that it was because of a physical infirmity that I first announced the gospel to you" (Gal 4:13–15) was meant specifically to address those readers/hearers who were at Derbe and not for all the south Galatian cities in general. All of them could not have seen him stricken with malaria and still travelling steadily onward.

To repeat: after those crises in Galatia, Jerusalem, and Antioch, Paul never returned to Antioch, and returned only once—faithfully, fatefully and fatally—to Jerusalem (*pace* Acts 18:22). But that final Jerusalem visit is a subject for this book's ultimate chapters. To complete this one, I turn from Paul's second, dependent, or Cypro-Anatolian Mission to his own third, independent, or Aegean Mission.

———————————◇————————————

For Luke-Acts, the Aegean Mission's starts—as did the preceding Cypro-Anatolian Mission (13:2,4)—under the Holy Spirit's control-and-command as part of the overall Spirit-controlled westward drive from Jerusalem to Rome (Acts 1:8; 19:21; 23:11):

> They [Paul and Timothy] went through the region of Phrygia and Galatia, having been forbidden by the Holy Spirit to speak the word in Asia. When they had come opposite Mysia, they attempted to go into Bithynia, but the Spirit of Jesus did not allow them; so, passing by Mysia, they went down to Troas. (Acts 16:6–8)

Alexandria-Troas was located about 10 miles north of Homer's fabled Ilion-Troy in the northwestern reaches of the Roman province of Asia Minor (on today's northern Aegean coast of Turkey). It was, by the way, an important enough port city and transit point between Asia and Europe that both Julius Caesar and Constantine considered it as a potential capital for the Roman Empire.

At Troas, of course, Paul and Timothy were already within Roman Asia Minor. Hence, silenced in Roman Asia and prevented from going northward to Roman Bithynia-Pontus by land, the only onward progress from Troas was to the Roman province of Macedonia by sea. In other words, they were already Spirit-controlled for that inaugural transition from Asia to Europe even without this following redundant revelation:

> During the night Paul had a vision: there stood a man of Macedonia pleading with him and saying, "Come over to Macedonia and help us." When he had seen the vision, we immediately tried to cross over to Macedonia, being convinced that God had called us to proclaim the good news to them. We set sail from Troas and took a straight course to Samothrace, the following day to Neapolis, and from there to Philippi, which is a leading city of the district of Macedonia and a Roman colony. (Acts 16:9–12)

(You will notice, of course, that abrupt transition from third-person *he* to first-person *we* in 16:10–17 and keep that in mind for much fuller discussion later in Chapter 11.) Instead, however, of any further westward progress, what happens next is a major southward "detour" through Roman Macedonia into Roman Achaia. Furthermore, that itinerary's city sequence is confirmed—in a rather striking agreement—by Paul himself.

Philippi:	Acts 16:12	=	1 Thess 2:2
Thessalonica:	Acts 17:1	=	1 Thess 1:5; 2:1,9
Athens:	Acts 17:15	=	1 Thess 3:1,6
Corinth:	Acts 18:1	=	1 Cor 1 & 2
[from Ephesus]			

As best we can see, therefore, Luke-Acts and Paul agree that the succession of Roman provincial foundations in his Aegean Mission was:

first Macedonia, for Philippi, Thessalonica—and also Beroea (16:12; 17:1,10); then Achaia, for Corinth (17:15; 18:1); and finally Asia, for Ephesus (18:19,21; 19:1).

A footnote. Luke-Acts knows Paul was at Ephesus but does not know for sure how he got there so he gives the reader two accounts—from opposite directions. In a first version, Paul comes eastward from Corinth to Ephesus by sea but he only "went into the synagogue . . . had a discussion with the Jews [and] when they asked him to stay longer, he declined" (18:19–20). In an immediate second version, Paul came westward from Antioch to Ephesus by land:

> On taking leave of them, he said, "I will return to you, if God wills." Then he set sail from Ephesus . . . landed at Caesarea . . . went up to Jerusalem . . . went down to Antioch. After spending some time there he departed and went from place to place through the region of Galatia and Phrygia, strengthening all the disciples . . . passed through the interior regions and came to Ephesus. (18:21–23; 19:1)

Furthermore, as you may recall, Luke had described Paul's first east-to-west arrival at Asian Troas as coming there "through the region of Phrygia and Galatia" (Acts 16:6). That same phrase was used—just above—as Paul arrives at Asian Ephesus "through the region of Galatia and Phrygia" (18:23).

In summary. Luke-Acts certainly knows Pauline sites and even some Pauline site-sequences. But for Ephesus, he either does not know how Paul got there, or, more likely, he does know that Paul got to Ephesus from west-to-east and rejects that as against his vision of *The Way of the Holy Spirit* heading steadily east-to-west toward Rome. In any case, we will have to look at that Aegean Mission once more in Chapters 10 and 11. For here and now, however, I turn to emphasize certain major continuity patterns between Paul's Cypro-Anatolian Mission under Barnabas and his own Aegean Mission after he broke with Barnabas.

The first continuity pattern concerns Jewish members and Gentile supporters in synagogues on the Sabbath. We met that combination at Pisidian Antioch as "God-fearers" (13:16,26) or "God-worshipers" (13:43,50). They reappear at:

> Philippi: "A certain woman named Lydia, a worshiper of God (*sebomēne ton theon*), was listening to us; she was from the city of Thyatira and a dealer in purple cloth. The Lord opened her heart to listen eagerly to what was said by Paul." (16:14)
>
> Thessalonica: "Some of them were persuaded and joined Paul and Silas, as did a great many of the devout Greeks (*sebomenōn Ellēnōn*) and not a few of the leading women." (17:4)
>
> Athens: "He argued in the synagogue with the Jews and the devout persons (*sebomenois*), and also in the market-place every day with those who happened to be there." (17:17)
>
> Corinth: "Then he left the synagogue and went to the house of a man named Titius Justus, a worshiper of God (*sebomenou ton theon*); his house was next door to the synagogue." (18:7)

Also, at Beroea (modern Veria)—about fifty miles southwest of Thessalonica on the Via Egnatia across the Balkans—that same distinction appears like this: "Many of them [the Jews] therefore believed, including not a few Greek women and men of high standing" (17:12). As he had learned from Barnabas, and even after his break with and from him at Antioch, Paul obviously retained those Gentile synagogue-sympathizers as the primary focus of his mission "among the Gentiles." The third or Aegean Mission retained that successful—if explosive—strategy from the second or Cypro-Anatolian Mission.

The second continuity pattern concerns that lethal response to any unacceptable Jew-and-Gentile combination. As seen already, this was established earlier with Jesus at Nazareth in Luke 4:16–30 and repeated with Paul at Pisidian Antioch in Acts 13:14–52. It now reappears in standard fourfold sequence at Thessalonica:

First, the proclamation of Jesus as Messiah: "They came to Thessalonica, where there was a synagogue of the Jews. And Paul went in, as was his custom, and on three sabbath days argued with them from the scriptures . . . 'This is the Messiah, Jesus whom I am proclaiming to you.'" (17:1–3)

Next, the initial Jewish reaction is positive: "Some of them were persuaded and joined Paul and Silas." (17:4a)

Then, the Gentile participation is mentioned: "as did a great many of the devout Greeks and not a few of the leading women." (17:4b)

Finally, the initial Jewish response turns lethal: "But the Jews became jealous, and with the help of some ruffians in the marketplaces they formed a mob and set the city in an uproar." (17:5)

Paul had made those Gentile sympathizers into a flash point within Sabbath synagogues. Did full male membership in the synagogue mean circumcision for males as had always been possible, or noncircumcision for males as Paul now claimed? And, what about women for whom circumcision was irrelevant? Were there more women than men among the Gentile supporters in most synagogues? An affirmative answer is indicated by what Josephus says about Gentile reactions of initial Jewish successes at the start of the Judeo-Roman war of 66–74:

> The people of Damascus . . . were fired with a determination to kill the Jews who resided among them . . . Their only fear was of their own wives who, with few exceptions, had all become converts (*hypēgmenas*) to the Jewish religion, and so their efforts were mainly directed to keeping the secret from them. (*JW* 2.559–261; *Life* 27)

Gentile synagogue-supporters knew that to become full members of God's people, they needed—if male—to be circumcised. But Paul insisted that they could be and should now be full members as uncircumcised Messianic/Christic Jews. The Sabbath synagogue thus became a struggle-site for the prize of those God-fearers/ worshipers.

The third and final continuity pattern concerns that hounding of Paul from city to city. We saw this earlier on his second or Cypro-Anatolian Mission at Lystra when "Jews came there from Antioch and Iconium and won over the crowds" (14:19). Luke-Acts continues that process in Europe as in Asia on Paul's third or Aegean Mission. From Thessalonica Paul continued to Beroea/Veria but when "the Jews of Thessalonica learned that the word of God had been proclaimed by Paul in Beroea as well, they came there too, to stir up and incite the crowds" (17:13). So Paul continued southward to Athens (Acts 17:16=1 Thess 3:1) and Corinth (Acts 18:1=1 Cor 1:14).

Watch, next, how that visionary focus and missionary shortcut on Gentiles/Greeks as God-fearers/God-worshipers clarify Paul's life and letters, Paul's plan and purpose, Paul's speed and passage— under four interactive aspects.

First, about Gentiles. Paul's focus on Gentile synagogue-supporters explains how his "Gentiles" understood him so readily—be it for agreement or disagreement. If those Gentiles were pure polytheists who knew little or nothing about Judaism or were even contemptuous or adverse to it, how could Paul convert them so swiftly and so completely? Would such candidates be capable of understanding, say, his letter to the Galatians? No oral instruction in passing would have sufficed to turn them first to monotheism, then, within monotheism, to the God of Judaism, and, finally, within the Jewish God to Jesus' fulfillment of its Messianic/Christic expectations. On the other hand, those God-worshipers had already accepted the God of Judaism and at least heard about its expected Messiah/Christ.

Second, about Jews. Paul's focus on Gentile synagogue-supporters explains why his fellow Jews were so inimical to Paul. Suppose, for example, that Paul at Corinth had converted pure Gentiles unconnected with Judaism or the synagogue. Suppose he had gone to those who worked the *Diolkos*, the 4-mile-long paved slipway that allowed boats to avoid the dangerous headlands of southern

Greece by being hauled across its middle between the Corinthian Gulf on the Ionian Sea and the Saronic Gulf on the Aegean. Why would pious Jews care if Paul converted such Gentiles to the Jewish God even with heretical Messianic/Christic theology? Why would Jews care if he told Gentiles to avoid circumcision or kosher, which Gentiles, of course, never had any intention of accepting? But imagine that message given to Gentiles listening with and seated among Jews in Sabbath-synagogues—imagine how explosive poaching such sympathizers and alienating such supporters would have been. Think of what happened at Pisidian Antioch, Iconium, and Lystra on the Cypro-Anatolian Mission (Acts 13:50; 14:1–5,19–20).

With internal Jewish strife in the synagogues becoming external urban turmoil in the streets, opposition to Paul explains his later admission of both Jewish and Roman punishments: "five times I have received from the Jews the forty lashes minus one. Three times I was beaten with rods. Once I received a stoning" (1 Cor 11:24–25).

Finally, but above all else, Paul's focus on the Gentile synagogue-supporters explains how he was able to move so swiftly, able to say in what turned out to be his final epistle that, "from Jerusalem and as far around as Illyricum I have fully proclaimed the good news of Christ . . . but now, with no further place for me in these regions, I desire, as I have for many years, to come to you" (Rom 15:19,23). Illyricum was the Roman name for our Yugoslavia, that once-upon-a-time confederation of the southern Slavic peoples inland along the eastern coast of the Adriatic Sea.

The phrase Jerusalem to Illyricum is Paul's Mediterranean-based geographical term for everything from Israel to Italy, that is, for the entire eastern half of the Roman Empire. That done, he is now going through Rome as a pivot to the western Roman Empire. He plans, "to come to you when I go to Spain. . . . I will set out by way of you to Spain" (Rom 15:23,24,28). How could Paul say he was finished with the eastern Roman Empire after about twenty missionary years?

Because, in terms of deliberate mission strategy, Paul did not go directly to the Forum to convert Gentiles but neither did he go to the synagogue to convert Jews. For Paul that would have been directly against his status as "Apostle of the Gentiles" mandated by visionary revelation in Damascus (Gal 1:15–16). Following Barnabas' strategy, Paul went to the synagogue because that was where on the Sabbath he could find God-worshipers as his Gentile candidates. We can surely see how explosive such synagogue-encroaching and sympathizer-poaching would have been, how deeply it would have divided those Gentile supporters, how seriously it would have infuriated Jewish authorities, and, worst of all, how easily any social turmoil would have attracted the attention of local Roman power. In any case, the Pauline train ran on God-worshiper rails; the Pauline express moved swiftly because it did not have to lay track.

I turn now from breadth to depth, from geography to theology, and from missionary strategy to missionary vision. How was life lived for Paul and, hopefully, for his communities, when they were no longer just waiting, praying, and hoping for the cosmic justification of this world as an imminent end-time product but were also participating, collaborating, and moving within it as a present in-time process? How were such lives even imagined in an actual world of Roman imperialism as Mediterranean globalization? How, in speech and rite, text and ritual, did Paul and his converts live resurrected lives religio-politically and socio-economically here on earth?

Chapter 8

"A NEW CREATION
IS EVERYTHING"

The sacred seventh day is . . . a relief and relaxation from labor
. . . not to free men only, but also to slaves, and even to beasts
of burden . . . even to every description of animal . . . and it af-
fects even every species of plant and tree; for there is no shoot,
and no branch, and no leaf even which it is allowed to cut or to
pluck on that day, nor any fruit which it is lawful to gather; but
everything is at liberty and in safety on that day, and enjoys, as
it were, perfect freedom.

—Philo, *Life of Moses*

Paul's vision of life in the new creation where resurrection was now an
in-time phenomenon even if it still—and soon—awaited an end-time
consummation, can be crystalized at the interface of text and ritual—
of a text in this chapter and of a ritual in the next one. Each is equally
grounded in the execution-resurrection of Jesus the Messiah/Christ
where, in the thesis of this book, that "resurrection" interpretation was
first created by Paul the Pharisee and is therefore not found anywhere
before him.

As you will recall from the start of Chapter 2, *The Gospel
according to Q* was the only gospel-version prior or contemporary with
The Gospel according to Paul but, in any case, independent of it. What,
however, was most striking in that textual comparison was that, while
the transcendent and cosmic reading of the execution-resurrection
of the Messiah/Christ was foundational for Paul, it was completely
absent from *Q* because irrelevant for *Q*.

I now turn, from *Q* as independent of Paul, to touch in this and
the next chapter on another source equally independent of Paul and

at least possibly as early as Paul. This is a disciplinary manual for community life whose main manuscript—copied in 1056—was only discovered by Metropolitan Bryennios of Nicomedia in the Patriarchal Library at Constantinople in 1873. After 150 years, that document is still as controversial as ever. A first warning of compositional puzzles to come is given immediately by that single text having twin titles: "The Teaching of the Twelve Apostles" and "The Teaching of the Lord through the Twelve Apostles to the Nations." Since teaching is *didachē* in Greek, this text's usual title is simply the *Didache*.

Here, however, is the *Didache*'s importance for this and the next chapter. Whether you date *Didache* to the second century because you judge its 1.3b–2.1 to be dependent on the *Q* material in Matt 5:39–48=Luke 6:27–36 (in the so-called Sermon on the Mount) or first century because you take it as independent from that material, the *Didache* does not even cite Jesus the Messiah/Christ as the source of that foundational teaching. Also, of course, it has nothing whatsoever of the execution-resurrection theology so basic to Paul. Only at the very end of text and time does it even mention "the resurrection of the dead ones (*anastasis nekrōn*)" in 16.6.

Here, to repeat, is the constitutive question about Paul as Pharisee: is the reason we do not find any execution-resurrection theology before Paul because it was precisely Paul the Messianic/Christic Pharisee who created it so that it came into the tradition from him alone? That would mean, of course, that it was *The Gospel according to Mark* that first combined the life-and-mission of the Messiah/Christ with the execution-and-resurrection of the Messiah/Christ to form the canonical gospel narrative that was then adopted and adapted by the other three versions of Mathew, Luke, and John.

The Pauline text to be probed in this chapter as a paradigmatic example of his vision is the letter that turned out to be Paul's last will and testament, a manifesto finale whose grand theme was "justification" (*dikaiosynē*), that is, the remaking of the world through a just distribution of creation for all creatures and an equitable share of earth's resources for all peoples.

Furthermore, that last and testimonial letter was written—appropriately—to the Romans whose imperial rulers considered that the justification of the world was their divine mandate, imperial destiny, general intention, and particular accomplishment (Virgil, *Aeneid* 1.278–283; 6.851–853).

In the New Testament, by the way, "justification" is a concept found only in Paul and important enough for him to use three different Greek words for it in Romans alone: *dikaiōsis* (4:25; 5:18); *dikiōma* (5:16); and *dikaiosynē* (5:21). With all of that in mind, I look now at Rom 8:14–23, in two sections, 14–17a and 19–23.

Romans 8:14–17a

This is a text that requires not just translation from one language to another but from one culture to another, or, better, from one world-vision to another—from civilization to post-civilization. I give it in parallel with Gal 4:3–7 because Paul, in recapitulating that earlier Galatians version in his later Romans one, made one small but telling change:

Table 2

Galatians 4:3–7	*Romans 8:14–17a*
While we were minors, we were enslaved to the elemental spirits (*stoicheia*) of the world. But when the fullness of time had come, God sent his Son (*huion*), born of a woman, born under the law, in order to redeem those who were under the law, so that we might receive sonship (*huiothesian*). And because you are sons (*huioi*), God has sent the Spirit of his Son (*huiou*) into our hearts, crying, "*Abba!* Father!" So you are no longer a slave but a son (*huios*), and if a son (*huios*) then also an heir, through God.	All who are led by the Spirit of God are sons (*huioi*) of God. For you did not receive a spirit of slavery to fall back into fear, but you have received a spirit of sonship (*huiothesias*). When we cry, "*Abba!* Father!" it is that very Spirit bearing witness with our spirit that we are children (*tekna*) of God, and if children (*tekna*), then heirs, heirs of God and co-heirs with Christ.

In those translations I have deliberately translated certain Greek words literally—against the NRSV—so you can see Paul's consistent use of son-language (*huios*) in Galatians but his shift from son-language to child-language (*teknon*) in Romans. There are three points in that text for discussion: first, Sons-and-Heirs; then, Father-and-Abba; and finally, Law-and-Slavery.

First, Sons-and-Heirs. In a patriarchal culture, with male primogeniture, terms such as "the son" or "the only son" or "the beloved son" or "the first-born son" designate the heir apparent—be it of family farm, royal realm, or cosmic power. It is conceptually inadequate to translate Paul's term "son" as "child" since "child" does not necessarily designate an "heir" and his invented word "sonship" can only be translated by our word "heirship."

When Paul recapitulated that Galatian text in Romans, he attempted to make that same "sonship/heirship" point while struggling more overtly and at least semi-successfully against the patriarchal prejudices that used "sons" to mean "heirs" and had only "sons" as "heirs." With "sons"-as-heirs and "sonship"-as-heirship established, Paul ends with a double mention of "children"-as-heirs. Vision struggles against culture and, whatever about Gal 4:3b–7, Rom 8:14–17a is at least a half-victory for vision: we are all heirs of God.

What is at stake behind Greek language and Roman culture is this profound challenge: Rome proclaims "sons (*huioi*)-as-heirs" in the culture of the Law's androcentrism; Paul proclaims the transition from "sons (*huioi*)-as-heirs" to "children (*tekna*)-as-heirs" in the culture of the Spirit's witness.

Next, Father-and-Abba. The historical Jesus used two megametaphors for his visionary message—the Family of God-as-Father and the Kingdom of God-as-Ruler—but the former was also the model for the latter. It was, for example, the distributive justice administered by the householder of the farmhouse—"the father" in patriarchal bias—feeding, clothing, sheltering, and protecting the children fairly and equitably, that modelled God—the Father by patriarchal bias—as the Householder of the World House operating similarly in transcendental analogy. You can glimpse Jesus' transition from farmhouse to world house in what we call "The Lord's Prayer" as it proceeds from "Our Father" to "Your kingdom come" (*Q* in Matthew 6:9=Luke 11:2).

In English, "Father" is the public title for the male parent and can be used by anyone but "Dad"—or some equivalent—is an intra-familial address that can only be rightfully used by a born child or an adopted child or a child's spouse—if and when invited to do so. That intra-familial address can and does hold even if and when a child is fully grown with fully grown children. The address "Dad" implies an unbreakable relationship between male parent and child but, in itself, does not indicate the speaker as infantile or childish but only as in-tractably bonded within a familial relationship.

Similarly, in Hebrew or Aramaic the neutral word *Ab* or *Aba* for Father generates an intra-familial address with *Abba*. When ad-dressed to God, *Abba* indicates no more but also no less than in-tra-familial status for the speaker, the status of being already within the Family of God-as-Father with all the rights and responsibilities inherent in that relationship. That ontological status arises because, as Paul says, "God has sent the Spirit of his Son into our hearts" (Gal 4:6). That makes recipients of that Spirit-transplant—in a carefully balanced and stunningly climactic expression—"heirs of God, co-heirs of Christ" (Rom 8:17, literal translation). Not sub-heirs, be it noted, but co-heirs.

Finally, Law-and-Slavery. For Paul here, "slavery" designates the existential situation of all human beings as such rather than the individual possession of some human beings by others. Humanity is "enslaved to the elemental spirits of the world" (Gal 4:3). In Greek, that term "elemental spirits" is simply "elements" (*stoicheia*) and it means the individual parts that make up any whole—for example, the letters that make up an alphabet.

For Paul, "elements/*stoicheia*" is a negative and dismissive term that designates the stuff of this world or, in my language, the nor-malcy of civilization, that is, everything that empowers, supports, defends, and protects our threefold war on environment, other spe-cies, and ourselves. The post-Pauline letter to the Colossians, for example, caught Paul perfectly when it asked rhetorically: "If with Christ you died to the elemental spirits of the universe (*stoicheia tou kosmou*), why are you dogmatized (*dogmatizesthe*) as if living in/by the world?" (2:20, literal translation). But how, in particular, is law a special part of our enslavement to the stuff of this world?

On the one hand, Paul insists that, "the law is holy, and the commandment is holy and just (*dikaia*) and good" (Rom 7:12). On the other, he is (in)famous for his denigration of law, especially when he counterpoints it with a celebration of grace: "you are not under law but under grace" (Rom 6:14). How is that to be explained?

(I am writing this in 2023, and, as Americans, imagine we are standing in front of the Supreme Court in Washington, DC, and looking up to read EQUAL JUSTICE UNDER LAW above the main entrance. At this moment in time, do we take that mantra's twin halves as redundancy or as oxymoron? Does UNDER LAW guarantee EQUAL JUSTICE or, by proclaiming it publicly, does UNDER LAW obviate the accomplishment and obstruct the fulfilment of EQUAL JUSTICE? If we think the latter, then we are ready—belatedly—to understand Paul on "law.")

Despite presumptions or assertions, "law" for Paul does not mean Jewish covenantal law in whole or in part, not especially so, not particularly so, and certainly not exclusively so. It would be more accurate to say that—especially, particularly, and certainly—"law" for Paul intended a focus on the vaunted Roman imperial law which had executed Jesus. All in all, however, "law" for Paul meant not just Jewish or Roman but human law as such. Paul's great intuition and searing conclusion is this: the purpose of law is the obstruction of justice, the effect of law is the circumvention of justice. Think about it.

Romans 8:19–23

After Paul recast Gal 4:3–7 into Rom 8:14–17a, he continued with a magnificent expansion in 8:19–23. For Paul then, or anyone else ever, what alternative is there to living with "the weak and beggarly elements of the world" (Gal 4:3,9)? What option is there to living—in my language—within the normalcy of civilization? Paul's answer is given in Rom 8:19–23, and here is that text in full so that you can see, as in that preceding Rom 8:14–18, that careful oscillation between gendered "sons-as-heirs" and ungendered "children-as-heirs":

> The creation waits with eager longing for the revealing of
> the sons (*huiōn*) of God; for the creation was subjected to

futility, not of its own will but by the will of the one who subjected it, in hope that the creation itself will be set free from its bondage to decay and will obtain the freedom of the glory of the children (*teknōn*) of God. We know that the whole creation has been groaning in labor pains until now; and not only the creation, but we ourselves, who have the first fruits of the Spirit, groan inwardly while we wait for sonship (*huiothesian*) the redemption of our bodies. (Rom 8:19–23; literal translation)

That text is a hymnic manifesto, a rhapsodic chant, and a visionary hope. In five verses, the word "creation" is used five times and the unit is framed with the terms "sons/sonship."

We and creation may "groan" alike in "labor pains until now." But while creation may sometimes make us "groan," Paul stresses rather how we have made creation "groan," made it subject to our own "bondage and decay."

There is, then, this obvious question: where did Paul get that vision of humanity as slaves within world (*kosmos*) but able to become heirs within creation (*ktisis*)? When he repeats the term "creation" like a drumbeat, what exactly does he mean by "creation"? The answer is that Rom 8:9–23 is Paul's reformulation of Gen 1:26–27: in creation, humans are created as images of God and in Romans they are recreated as heirs of God. But humans are—or should be by identity and destiny—images or heirs precisely as stewards of creation for the God of the Sabbath (Gen 1:26–2:4a). But why is that last term so important for creation?

When the biblical tradition was assembled formally after the return from Babylonian Exile in the later 500s BCE, that Genesis text was composed as the prologue through which to view the whole that followed it. A God who could have created with a single "Let the world be," deliberately and obviously used eight individual, and separate, and cumulative "let this-or-that be"s (1:3,6,9,11,14,20,24,26); but those eight "let this-or-that be"s are obviously packed into six days with one "let-be" on Days 1,2,4, and 5 (1:3,6,14,20) but two "let-be"s on Days 3 and 6 (1:9,11,24,26). Those six days are then balanced between three days of Preparing "the heavens and the earth"

(1:3–13) and three days of Presenting "all their multitude" (1:14–31). That carefully calibrated metaphor of a *week for creation* ensured that the crown of creation would be the seventh or Sabbath day of rest. (We are not the crown of creation. We are the work of a late Friday afternoon, a time when best work is seldom done.)

Within the poetics of that scenario, humanity—female and male—was created "in the image and likeness of God," that is to say, humanity was created as stewards and representatives of the Sabbath God for the management of the Sabbath God's creation (1:26–27). Genesis called humanity an image of God and Paul called it an heir of God but both terms designate our existential identity and ontological destiny.

The God of Genesis 1 is a God of distributive justice not just by decree, commandment, or external law for humanity but by existence, character, and internal being from divinity. That is why Creation meant that existence was distributed fairly to the whole universe by divinity, and Sabbath meant that the universe's existence was to be maintained as fairly distributed by humanity. Also, with Sabbath Rest/Freedom as the crown of creation, time itself was established by and attuned to the rhythm of distributive justice as Sabbath Days, Sabbath Years, and Sabbath Jubilees established days and weeks, months, years, and centuries.

First, the Sabbath Day meant that rest was the primordial and paradigmatic right of all creatures from creation itself: "Six days you shall do your work, but on the seventh day you shall rest, so that your ox and your donkey may have relief, and your homeborn slave and the resident alien may be refreshed" (Exod 23:12). That right of rest was addressed to the Parents of Israel: "you, or your son or your daughter, or your male or female slave, or your ox or your donkey, or any of your livestock, or the resident alien in your towns, so that your male and female slave may rest as well as you" (Deut 5:12–15).

In case rest as the basis of cosmic justification sounds trite to those of us privileged to have had rest always built into our jobs or careers, lives or times, read again that quotation from Philo used as epigraph for this chapter. There, the Sabbath Day starts as rest-from, "relief and relaxation from labor," and ends as rest-for "liberty and safety . . . and . . . perfect freedom" (*Life of Moses* 2.4,21-22). Think, therefore, about rest-for-freedom building the basis of cosmic justification into the structure of time itself as Sabbath Creation expands from Sabbath Day through Sabbath Year to Sabbath Jubilee. The Sabbath Day's rest might seem so little until you explore it, but, then, so is an atom until you explode it.

Next, the Sabbath Year involved two different areas of special rest-from-labor and special rest-for-freedom. One was freedom from cultivation for the land itself:

> For six years you shall sow your land and gather in its yield; but the seventh year you shall let it rest and lie fallow, so that the poor of your people may eat; and what they leave the wild animals may eat. You shall do the same with your vineyard, and with your olive orchard. (Exod 23:10–11)

Letting the land "lie fallow" periodically is prudent agricultural procedure to allow its replenishment of minerals, moisture, and microbes—and also to give the farmer a rest. But the reason given for this divine command—the "so that . . ."—is to benefit, by right of creation, first the poor, and then the wild animals.

In Leviticus, that seventh-year rest for the land itself is emphasized much more than in Exodus: "the land shall observe a sabbath . . . a sabbath of complete rest for the land . . . a year of complete rest for the land" (25:2,4,5). Only after that triple repetition of rest/freedom for the land itself, does it conclude:

> You may eat what the land yields during its sabbath—you, your male and female slaves, your hired and your bound laborers who live with you; for your livestock also, and for the wild animals in your land all its yield shall be for food. (Lev 25:6–7)

You will recognize the special concern for the most vulnerable categories among humans and animals alike.

The other special area concerns rest/freedom from debt and debt-slavery. Absent a full slave-economy based on conquest in war, an individual could become a slave to pay off a debt or protect the family farm from foreclosure as collateral for an unpaid one.

First, with regard to rest/freedom from debt every seventh year, "you shall grant a remission of debts . . . every creditor shall remit the claim that is held against a neighbor . . . who is a member of the community." (Since foreigners do not give such debt-release, neither do they get it.) There is also a warning against refusing all loans because of that injunction: "I therefore command you, 'Open your hand to the poor and needy neighbor in your land'" (Deut 15:1–11).

Next, with regard to freedom from debt-slavery every seventh year, there are special gender-based provisions for males or females so enslaved: "When you send a male slave out from you a free person, you shall not send him out empty-handed. Provide liberally out of your flock, your threshing floor, and your wine press . . . because for six years they have given you services worth the wages of hired laborers" (Deut 15:13–14). Even as pure theory, that is an extraordinary command to treat a seven-year debt-slave at release as if he had been a hired worker all along.

There are four conditions "when a man sells his daughter as a slave" and she has been taken into the household as a potential wife:

> If she does not please her master, who designated her for himself, then he shall let her be redeemed; he shall have no right to sell her to a foreign people, since he has dealt unfairly with her.
>
> If he designates her for his son, he shall deal with her as with a daughter.
>
> If he takes another wife to himself, he shall not diminish the food, clothing, or marital rights of the first wife.
>
> If he does not do these three things for her, she shall go out without debt, without payment of money. (Exod 21:8–11)

The rest/freedom of the Sabbath Day was a creational and constitutional right that extended through those Sabbath Years into its consummation in the fiftieth year after seven Sabbath Years.

Finally, that Sabbath Jubilee was a Super-Sabbath-Year. That included all the usual Sabbath Year restrictions: "you shall not sow, or reap the aftergrowth, or harvest the unpruned vines . . . you shall eat only what the field itself produces" (Lev 25:11–12). But that Jubilee Year demanded one other even more powerful rest/freedom from systemic and structural, social and economic injustice: "you shall return, every one of you, to your property and every one of you to your family . . . you shall return, every one of you, to your property" (25:10,13).

The theory behind that rest/freedom from land acquisition is quite stunning, with God speaking: "the land shall not be sold in perpetuity, for the land is mine; with me you are but aliens and tenants" (25:23). Originally God's land was distributed by God fairly and equitably among the tribes and families of Israel. But then came "you who join house to house, who add field to field, until there is room for no one but you, and you are left to live alone in the midst of the land!" (Isaiah 58). That greed is why the Sabbath Jubilee Year must start precisely "on the Day of Atonement" (Lev 25:9).

From humans as images of God in Gen 1:26–27 to humans as heirs of God in Rom 8:14–23, Paul recapitulates what he had written twice already: "a new creation is everything" (Gal 6:15) and "if anyone is in Christ, there is a new creation: everything old has passed away; see, everything has become new" (2 Cor 5:17). By the way, that phrase *a new creation* is unique to Paul in the New Testament and is what I call post-civilization.

We can, as always, read that "new creation" within the biblical tradition of the Supreme God and/or the evolutionary tradition of the Big Bang. We can think of ourselves as images or heirs of God and/or of Evolution. But, still and so far, the evidence is that our species, *Homo sapiens*, left Africa around 70,000 years ago, eradicated all other hominid species that emigrated before we did, and started our onslaught on creation under the war-banner of civilization.

As the only species that knows about evolution, we recognize that civilization makes us the most endangering and endangered species on earth; that we look back to pre-civilization as a past we cannot renew; and to post-civilization as a future we cannot imagine. If you are a theist, you should think of Paul's new creation of post-civilization working from God but through Evolution. If you are an atheist, you should think of Paul's new creation of post-civilization working through Evolution. Whether or not the ultimate challenge is God, the proximate challenge is Evolution. Whether or not there are sanctions from God, there are certainly ones from Evolution—already overtly operational.

Chapter 9

"WE HAVE DIED WITH CHRIST"

> What does it mean to live in the Messiah, and what is the messianic life? What is the structure of messianic time? These questions, meaning Paul's questions, must also be ours. . . . Messianic time . . . is not the line of chronological time . . . nor the instant of its end . . . it is operational time pressing within the chronological time, working and transforming it from within. . . . Messianic time is neither the complete nor the incomplete, neither the last nor the future, but the inversion of both.
>
> —Giorgio Agamben, *The Time that Remains*

I turn now from that preceding and paradigmatic text in Paul to a paradigmatic ritual in Paul—starting with Pauline texts about that ritual. I focus on baptism as the ritual of initiation into Paul's Messianic/Christic community as "the church (*ekklesia*) of God."

A ritual of initiation may either welcome you into the surrounding society as a part of the whole or welcome you out as a part against the whole. It may integrate you into cultural normalcy, officially and communally, civilly and politically, or separate you ceremonially and communally, religiously and theologically into counter-cultural resistance. The rite or ceremony of initiation both symbolizes and effects that transition—in either direction and to whatever status.

(In September of 1950, for example, I entered a thirteenth-century Roman Catholic mendicant or semi-cloistered religious order and the initiation ceremony involved public, official, and ceremonial re-nomination and re-vestition. My name was John Crossan and it was changed to Brother Dominic—based on the biblical tradition that a new vocation erased your past and gave you only a new future. My ordinary external dress of jacket and tie was replaced by a religious habit of soutane and belt, scapular and cowl—based on a stylized version of medieval peasant clothing. After that initiation, we novices were taught to consider ourselves "out of this world." In October of 1951, my religious superiors sent me to America on the Queen Mary—second class, hence no Ellis Island—and that, admittedly, was "out of this world.")

In the *Didache*—recall it from the start of the last chapter—this is the ritual for initiation: "Concerning baptism, baptize thus: Having first rehearsed all these things, 'baptize in the Name of the Father and of the Son and of the Holy Spirit'" (7.1a; from Jesus' departing words in Matt 28:19). But granted that baptism involved water the only further discussion is on running versus stationary water, cold versus warm water, water-immersion versus water-aspersion, and preparatory fasting (7:1b–4).

That teaching, however, was not very clear on why water of any sort was involved in that once-and-forever initiation—unlike Jewish repeated ritual washings. Maybe: a physical erasure of dirt from the body by water externally symbolized the erasure of sin from the soul by repentance? Maybe: since creation had involved "a wind from God sweeping over the face of the waters" (Gen 1:2), water baptism symbolized a new creation? In any case, there is nothing that even hints of Paul's execution-resurrection theology in the *Didache*'s presumably pre-Pauline initiation rite.

Be that as it may, how did the identity shift or spirit transplant required for this new creation work symbolically and effectively for Paul's initiates at baptism? I look at that process in three places where the subject arose for Paul and set it up therefore as three ever-deepening probes through the fundamentals of Paul's theology into the foundations of Paul's vision.

A First Probe

In 1 Cor 1:12–4:6, Paul was confronted with a quarrel over baptism that might seem rather trivial at first sight. But that subject also starts, continues, and concludes over what is for us the first four chapters of 1 Corinthians:

> Each of you says, "I belong to Paul," or "I belong to Apollos," or "I belong to Cephas," or "I belong to Christ." (1:12)

> When one says, "I belong to Paul," and another, "I belong to Apollos," are you not merely human? (3:4)
>
> Let no one boast about human leaders. For all things are yours, whether Paul or Apollos or Cephas or the world or life or death or the present or the future—all belong to you and you belong to Christ, and Christ belongs to God. (3:21–23)

Some Corinthian baptizands represented themselves as clients to their baptizers as patrons, and such top-down relationships were dragging Messianic/Christic theology back into the normalcy of traditional Greco-Roman culture. (Patronage-and-clientage has been described as the moral glue of the Mediterranean world, holding it all together with little-or-large pyramids of unequal power.)

In response, Paul criticized that surface quarrel from the deepest levels of his theology and applied it all "to Apollos and myself for your benefit" (4:6). He began by claiming that he at least had baptized very few at Corinth because "Christ did not send me to baptize but to proclaim the gospel, and not with eloquent wisdom, so that the cross of Christ might not be emptied of its power" (1:17). After that opening, he continued point/counterpoint to turn Greco-Roman culture upside down and shake up its brains, turn it inside out and shake out its entrails. But, as you read the serried dichotomies of his manifesto, it is clearly more profound than simply Messianic/Christic life as opposed to Greco-Roman culture; it is the new creation's alternative to the old creation's normalcy; it is post-civilization's challenge to civilization itself.

First, Paul opposed wisdom to folly (1:18–31; 3:18–20) and their admiration for superiority against his acceptance of inferiority (4:7–13). Next, he opposed power to weakness (1:26–31) and their admiration for oratory against his acceptance of ecstasy (2:1–5). Then, comes the revolution in those normal dichotomies: what divinity accepts as power and wisdom, humanity considers weakness and folly; what humanity accepts as power and wisdom, divinity considers weakness and folly (1:20b; 3:19). And here, climactically, is the powerful and eternal wisdom of God:

> Among the mature we do speak wisdom, though it is not
> a wisdom of this age or of the rulers of this age, who are
> doomed to perish. But we speak God's wisdom, secret
> and hidden, which God decreed before the ages for our
> glory. None of the rulers of this age understood this; for
> if they had, they would not have crucified the Lord of
> glory. . . . These things God has revealed to us through
> the Spirit; for the Spirit searches everything, even the
> depths of God. (2:6–10)

For Paul, the secret divine wisdom was God's justification of creation
by changing the end-time resurrecting-judging-sanctioning event
(*anastasis nekrōn*) into an in-time process after and because of civilization's public, official, and legal execution of Jesus the Messiah/
Christ, the Son of God, the Lord of glory.

Jesus lived and died for nonviolent resistance to the normal
violence of civilization. In that time and place, divinely modeled nonviolence was incarnated in Jesus and both he and it were officially rejected, publicly despised, and legally executed by imperially mandated
violence incarnated in Pilate. (So, then, what price law?) But only
nonviolent resistance can at least slow the escalatory normalcy of
humanity's three-front violence against the earth. So when Paul asked
then, "where is the one who is wise?" (1 Cor 1:20), we ask now, where
is the wisdom of *Homo sapiens*, the wisdom of Homo the Wise?

A Second Probe

In Rom 6:3–8, Paul returned to that just-seen grounding of baptism
in the crucifixion of Jesus (1 Cor 2:8) but now within the full Pauline
dyad of crucifixion-and-resurrection. First, watch the fourfold repetition as baptizands participate in the death and life/resurrection of
Christ:

> Do you not know that all of us who have been bap-
> tized into Christ Jesus were baptized into his death?
> Therefore we have been buried with him by baptism
> into death, so that, just as Christ was raised from the dead

by the glory of the Father, so we too might walk in newness of life.

For if we have been united with him in a death like his,
we will certainly be united with him in a resurrection like
his.

But if we have died with Christ, we believe that we will
also live with him. (6:3-5,8)

But what exactly does that mean, how exactly does that participation work, and why does "death" remain constant but "life/live" and
"raised/resurrection" alternate?

Paul is not describing baptism as a ritual commitment and symbolic death in preparation for the inevitable death of martyrdom—
like Jesus. Still, even granted that, I wonder about that fourfold emphasis on death. Why did Paul not simply say that "all of us who have
been baptized into Christ Jesus were baptized into his life?" Because,
for Paul, Jesus the Messiah/Christ died from the imperial values of
Roman normalcy which were, of course and to repeat, the normalcy
of civilization in first-century time, Mediterranean place, and togate
dress. But, in baptism, Messianic/Christics died not by that Rome
which had killed Jesus but to that Rome which had killed him. Thereafter, in the face of Rome as civilization's normalcy, they "walked in
newness of life" here on earth, that is, they lived resurrected lives in
the new creation, between the start and consummation of the general
resurrection.

My suggestion is that, for Paul, baptizands died to what Jesus
had died from, namely, the way of this world—as just seen in Rom
6:3–5,8. That is confirmed immediately by his emphasis on "sin"
intertwined with that section in 6:6–7,10–11:

Our old self was crucified with him so that the body
of sin might be destroyed, and we might no longer be
enslaved to sin. For whoever has died is freed from sin.
The death he died, he died to sin, once for all; but the
life he lives, he lives to God. So you also must consider
yourselves dead to sin and alive to God in Christ Jesus.
(6:6–7,10–11)

Focus on that claim whereby the baptizands' death to sin ("you") participates in Christ's death to sin ("he"). If you think of death to sin as the abandonment of one's sinful life, how can that apply to Paul's Jesus the Messiah/Christ? What then did Christ's "death to sin" mean for Paul?

For Paul, death is not the normal end of human life but the abnormal start of human civilization. As he put it, "the wages of sin is death" (Rom 6:23), and those wages were paid by God to Adam in Eden. For Paul, in other words, sin, and its concomitant result death, did not come from God's creation of world but from Adam's creation of counter-world. But, of course, "as all die in Adam, so all will be made alive in Christ," (1 Cor 15:22), and that, precisely, was what baptism effected. In my language, and whatever about death arising inaugurally from sin, Adam gave us civilization, Christ gave us post-civilization.

(One footnote. Recall this from Paul on Adam: "sin came into the world through one man, and death came through sin, and so death spread to all because [*eph' ho*] all have sinned" [Rom 5:12]. That did not mean "original sin" as an inevitable genetic culpability but only as an inevitable mimetic propensity. Here, from that same first century, are two other Jewish authors on Adam as our inaugural and ancestral bad example: "O Adam what have you done? For though it was you who sinned, the fall was not yours alone, but ours also who are your descendants" [4 Ezra 7:48]; and, "Adam is, therefore, not the cause, except only for himself, but each of us has become our own Adam" [2 Baruch 54:19].)

Granted all of that, however, there is a far stronger confirmation that it was by and from the normalcy of civilization that Christ died and that it was to and against it that Paul's baptizands "walked in newness of life." That confirmation is the subject of the next step in this ongoing probe into the core of Pauline theology.

A Third Probe

For Paul, what precisely are the normalcies of civilization by which Jesus died historically and really but to which Paul's baptizands died symbolically—but really? Here is a first account in Gal 3:27–28:

> As many of you as were baptized into Christ have clothed
> yourselves with Christ.
> > There is no longer Jew or Greek,
> > there is no longer slave or free,
> > there is no longer male and female;
> for all of you are one in Christ Jesus.

There is also a later and shorter version of that ritual chant proclaiming that, "in the one Spirit we were all baptized into one body—Jews or Greeks, slaves or free—and we were all made to drink of one Spirit" (1 Cor 12:13). The metaphor is now "drinking" rather than "clothing" and the frames are now "in/of—one Spirit" rather than "into/in—Christ.

At stake for Paul in those baptismal specifics was the delicate interface where difference and diversity became then—and still become now—hierarchy and discrimination. And become such, all too often, not as a prejudice of culture but as a postulate of nature. But, for Paul, why precisely those three dyads of Greek/Jew, Free/Slave, and Male/Female? Are they exclusive or representative and, if the latter, how and why so representative?

Stephen J. Patterson[1] of Oregon's Willamette University asked that exact question, "Why these three pairs in particular?" He answered that they represent, "a fairly complete accounting of the ways by which human beings divide themselves into us and them: race, class, and gender" (page 31). In fact, as he indicates, that same triple discrimination goes back to the Greek philosopher Aristotle's *Politics* from around 350 BCE.

First, with regard to race or ethnicity and the alleged natural ascendancy of Greek over Barbarian: "Among barbarians the female and the slave have the same rank; and the cause of this is that barbarians have no class of natural (*physei*) rulers, but with them the conjugal partnership is a partnership of female slave and male slave. Hence the saying of the poets, 'Tis meet that Greeks should rule

---

[1] Stephen J. Patterson, *The Forgotten Creed: Christianity's Original Struggle against Bigotry, Slavery, and Sexism.* Oxford, UK: Oxford University, Press. 2018.

barbarians,' implying that barbarian and slave are the same in nature (*physei*)." Later, he returned to its "natural character" (*physin*) whereby Greece "continues . . . to be capable of ruling all mankind if it attains constitutional unity" (1.1252b; 5.1327b).

Next, with regard to gender and the alleged natural ascendancy of Male over Female: "Again, as between the sexes, the male is by nature (*physei*) superior and the female inferior, the male ruler and the female subject" (1.1254b). Earlier he had proposed that "the household in its perfect form consists of slaves and freemen. The investigation of everything should begin with its smallest parts, and the primary and smallest parts of the household are master and slave, husband and wife, father and children" (1.1253b).

Finally, with regard to class and the alleged natural ascendancy of Master over Slave: Aristotle admits that there is disagreement on this subject. "Others however maintain that for one man to be another man's master is contrary to nature (*para physin*), because it is only convention that makes the one a slave and the other a freeman and there is no difference between them by nature (*physei*), and that therefore it is unjust, for it is based on force" (1.1253b). And again: "It is not difficult to see that those who assert the opposite are also right in a manner. The fact is that the terms 'slavery' and 'slave' are ambiguous; for there is also such a thing as a slave or a man that is in slavery by law, for the law is a sort of agreement under which the things conquered in war are said to belong to their conquerors" (1.1255a). Also, Aristotle admits that "we must next consider whether or not anyone exists who is by nature (*physei*) of this character, and whether it is advantageous and just for anyone to be a slave, or whether on the contrary all slavery is against nature (*para physin*)" (1.1254a).

Still, Aristotle's own view is as persistent as it is unpersuasive. He argues that "the nature of the slave and his essential quality" is that of "one who is a human being belonging by nature (*physei*) not to himself but to another;" that, "he is by nature (*physei*) a slave who is capable of belonging to another (and that is why he does so belong), and who participates in reason so far as to apprehend it but not to possess it;" that, "there are cases of people of whom some are freemen and the others slaves by nature (*physei*), and for these slavery is an institution both expedient and just" (1.1254a, 1254b, 1255a).

In summary. Anyone eventually enslaved by the law of conquest is thereby shown to have been already and always a slave by the law of nature.

If you read straight through *Politics* 1.1252a–1255b, three aspects are rather striking. One is that the hierarchy of class, that is, of slavery as the possession of "living tools," is the general matrix within which the other discriminants of race and gender are mentioned—almost in passing. Another is that, since slaves are so by nature, those enslaved by war must have been covertly slaves by nature all along! A final one is that Aristotle does not justify his threefold ascendancy as developed by custom, culture, or even history but as given "by nature" (*physei*) or "according to nature" (*kata physin*), with the opposite therefore "against nature" (*para physin*). Try, for example, to count the number of times "nature" is cited in *Politics* 1.1252a–1255b as if repeated assertion could change the customs of culture into the demands of nature. As I turn now from Aristotle to Paul, I take from the former into the latter an extremely critical skepticism about habits of culture masquerading as dictates of nature.

————⊹⊱✦⊰⊹————

On the one hand, Paul flatly contradicted Aristotle. In the old creation that triple distinction of race, class, and gender begot discrimination, inequality, and injustice. In the new creation, baptism committed baptizands to reject such difference-become-hierarchy because of their overwhelming oneness in God's Christ and their transcendent unity in God's Spirit. In such a community, differences become indifferent.

On the other hand, there remains that fundamental Aristotelian error of confusing culture with nature and his constant drumbeat of judging culture "by nature" (*physei*). The irony is that Paul himself gives two examples—one minor and one major—of that same confusion of by-culture as being by-nature (*physei*) and of judging what is against culture as being against nature (*para physin*).

The minor example happened at Corinth and concerned both a local problem hard to reconstruct and a Pauline response hard to justify. First, about his celibacy, Paul's personal example at Corinth and his declared principle for Corinth was that "I wish that all were as

I myself am. But each has a particular gift from God, one having one kind and another a different kind" (1 Cor 7:7). Next, based on that Pauline example, some Corinthian wives decided that "'It is well for a man not to touch a woman'" and proclaimed themselves as married celibates (7:1–6). Furthermore, in leading the community in prayer or prophecy, they proclaimed their status as celibate wives by rejecting the standard veil of the married matron for the unveiled hair of the unmarried virgin (11:5,13).

In rejecting that witness, Paul tried desperately to balance evenly the mutual obligations and relationships of the male/female dyad—using it twelve times in 1 Cor 11:4–15. One of them is even a flat contradiction to Gen 1:26–27: "a man . . . is the image and glory of God; but woman is the glory of man" (11:7). More importantly for here, however, is another of those balanced dyads in this rhetorical question: "Does not nature (*physis*) itself teach you that if a man wears long hair, it is degrading to him, but if a woman has long hair, it is her glory? (11:14–15a).

Surely, however, short hair for men and long hair for women are, wherever expected or whenever demanded, a cultural and not a natural distinction. Paul, himself, almost admits that with his final argument: "if anyone is disposed to be contentious—we have no such custom, nor do the churches of God" (11:16). Custom, however, be it accepted or rejected, is cultural and not natural.

The major example of that culture/nature confusion appeared in Romans and concerned same-sex intercourse. The law in Leviticus is that: "You shall not lie with a male as with a woman; it is an abomination" (18:22); and again: "If a man lies with a male as with a woman, both of them have committed an abomination; they shall be put to death; their blood is upon them" (20:13). Paul, however, decries same-sex intercourse for both women as well as men as found among Gentiles: "Their women exchanged natural (*physikēn*) intercourse for unnatural (*para physin*), and in the same way also the men, giving up natural intercourse (*physikēn*) with women, were consumed with passion for one another" (Rom 1:26b–27a).

The biblical tradition in Leviticus spoke only of male-with-male union and did not use the term "unnatural." Why, then, did

Paul mention both female-with-female and male-with-male and cite both as "unnatural"?

As scholars have shown, he did so because he was following not that biblical tradition from Leviticus but the philosophical one from Plato. In his last treatise, the *Laws*, Plato argued there that the "natural" (*kata physin*) purpose of female-with-male intercourse was procreation and that, therefore, it was "contrary to nature (*para physin*) when it was male-with-male or female-with-female" (*Laws* 1.636c). Also, for Plato, sexual pleasure was "granted by nature" only within that procreative intention and never outside it—even for married couples (*Laws* 1.636c).

Adapting Greek into Jewish tradition, the philosopher Philo agreed that the "natural" purpose of intercourse was procreation and that the human intention for intercourse should be equally exclusive to procreation. Therefore, for example, Philo judged husbands who knowingly married barren wives to be "enemies of nature" since they knew procreation was impossible (*The Special Laws* 3.36).

That same presumption that intercourse is "naturally" for procreation appears in the Jewish historian Josephus: "The Law recognizes no sexual connections, except the natural (*kata physin*) union of man and wife, and that only for the procreation of children. Sodomy it abhors, and punishes any guilty of such assaults with death" (*Against Apion* 2.199). The Greeks, on the contrary "attributed to the gods the practice of sodomy . . . thus inventing an excuse for the monstrous and unnatural (*para physin*) pleasures in which they themselves indulged" (2.275).

On the one hand, in Rom 1:16b–17a, Paul simply used the standard Jewish synagogue teaching that what was "natural" was married-intercourse-for-procreation-only so that all else was "unnatural" and he used it as a general accusation against the Gentile world. On the other, speaking to the Corinthians, he advised married intercourse not for procreation but simply "so that Satan may not tempt you because of your lack of self-control." Also, since, "the present form of this world is passing away," procreation and/or pleasure is somewhat irrelevant (1 Cor 7:5,31).

In any case, intercourse-for-procreation-only is not demanded by "nature" since—from nature—procreation and pleasure are twin but separable effects of intercourse. Nature allows procreation without pleasure, pleasure without procreation, either, neither, or both—and that is what we must rethink as "natural" in reading Paul.

Paul rejected the value of distinction and the validity of discrimination concerning race, class, and gender but he then introduced two other ones with hair length and sexual preference. All of that points to two even more fundamental challenges. One is our human tendency to confuse culture with nature, to claim as natural, inevitable, and unavoidable what is actually cultural, accidental, and mutable. Another is our human tendency to focus that cultural/natural confusion primarily or exclusively on sex rather than on violence, that is, on sex as covert distraction or overt focus away from violence. In any case, it might be well to worry less about "unnatural" sex and more about "unnatural" violence as we look to the future of our species on this earth.

A Final Probe

At the time of Paul's baptismal theology, his communities had no buildings dedicated as churches and no material structures for baptisms. When then we first find such designated baptismal structures, do they look like physical investments of Paul's baptismal theology—in part or in whole?

The very first baptismal structure still extant was discovered in a garrison town high on the western bank of the Euphrates on the frontier between the Roman and the Persian Empires. That fort's bilingual name, Dura-Europos, was already indicative of its precarious, east-west, trip-wire situation. In 256 CE, protected by the river from the east but now threatened by the Persia's Sasanian dynasty surrounding it from the west, the military garrison filled in the street behind the western wall and, although that failed to preserve their besieged lives, it did preserve those buried buildings. Among them was an ordinary dwelling house renovated to form a church-building around 240. In this unique pre-Constantinian baptistery, the baptismal structure itself was buried under and preserved by that earth-packed western wall—along with the murals that decorated the room.

In his study of that baptistery, Michael Peppard[2] noted that, in the first four centuries, Origen of Alexandria (185–244) was the first and only eastern theologian to interpret baptism as participation in Christ's death and resurrection, as Paul did in Rom 6:3–5. Hence, "one of the 'big stories' of pre-Nicene art and ritual is the stunning lack of emphasis—judged against the evidence of later centuries—on the imagery of Christ's death" (pages 55, 121). Against that patristic background, Peppard insists:

> Contrary to commonly held assumptions about early Christian initiation, the rituals at Dura-Europos did not primarily embody notions of death and resurrection.
>
> Paul's portrayal of baptism as death and resurrection with Christ has been influential throughout Christian history. In this baptistery, however, the only signified death is that of Goliath.
>
> For most of Christian history, the Pauline interpretation of baptism as death and resurrection has been dominant.
>
> In my overall interpretation of the artistic and ritual program of the Dura-Europos baptistery, these Christians emphasized salvation as victory, empowerment, healing, refreshment, marriage, illumination, and incarnation more than participation in a ritualized death. (pages 45, 89, 119–120, 198)

Still, even granted those conclusions from the artistic imagery on the baptistery's walls, what about the material shape of the baptismal structure itself since "the font was big enough for a person to stand or kneel in, but not big enough for full adult immersion" (page 141)? Is that structure a symbolic bath or a symbolic sarcophagus, either, neither, or both? In any case, and whatever about that pre-Constantinian baptismal structure, it is Paul's vision that is structurally invested in the

---

[2] Michael Peppard, *The World's Oldest Church* (New Haven, CT: Yale University Press, 2016), 45-198. The content below was downloaded from JSTOR through DePaul University, on May 27, 2023, at 4:15 p.m.

post-Constantinian world of dedicated churches with materially symbolic structures for baptism.

From the fourth century, for example, Our Lady's Church of the Hundred Gates (*Panagia Ekatontapiliani*), on the Greek island of Paros, does not have a hundred doors but it does have a baptismal structure shaped materially like a cruciform sarcophagus built up on the floor of the baptistery with steps down and up at opposite two of its four equal arms.

Also, for another example, the sixth-century Basilica of Saint John, in the Turkish town of Selçuk near Ephesus, has again a cruciform baptismal structure but dug down like a grave into the floor of the baptistery. And, again there were steps down and up at either end of the long shaft.

Furthermore, apart from those multiplied cruciform baptismal structures with step-in-down at one end and step-up-out at the other that are still in situ around the eastern Mediterranean, there are also, for example, two re-dug into the floor of the Bardo Museum in Tunis—one in rather starkly undecorated concrete, the other in magnificently decorated mosaic.

Finally, what exactly is of importance in that post-Constantinian material embodiment of Rom 6:3–5 in those baptismal structures shaped as cruciform "graves" or "sarcophagi" multiplied in situ or museums around the eastern Mediterranean—from Turkey to Tunisia? It is perfectly true—as Peppard emphasized—that symbols have meanings that differ and multiply across time and space, use, and perception. But, with polyvalence comes the possibility—however judged—that a given meaning can be good or bad, adequate or inadequate, old, outdated, renewed, or simply new.

If water-and-font symbolizes a washing away of personal and individual sin, it would leave untouched the structural and systemic sin of "this world" where the normalcy of civilization's rule of law "crucified the Lord of glory" (1 Cor 2:8). When, however, baptismal water is that of Gen 1:2 when "a wind from God swept over the face of the waters," baptism involves collaboration with and participation in a "new creation."

A "new creation" involves cosmic regeneration, that is, the radical renewal of the world's religious, political, social, and economic existence. But why would anyone ever imagine that the "old creation" would go quietly into the good light of a "new creation"? Paul certainly did not and his baptismal symbolism stated clearly that the baptizand died to what Jesus had died from, namely, the normalcy of civilization in empurpled Roman dress.

One final point to this chapter. Jesus' most famously explosive aphorism is "love your enemies," from *The Gospel according to Q* in Matt 5:44=Luke 6:27. Why did Jesus say "enemies" rather than "everyone" which would have implicitly included "enemies" without explicitly specifying them alone? Because Jesus knew that his vision of the Kingdom of God, that is, of God's Rule on Earth, was of human nonviolent resistance based on the nature or character of God (Q in Matt 5:45=Luke 6:35).

Jesus' position was summed up perfectly in that powerful parable when he was imagined as addressing Pilate with this challenge: "My kingdom is not from this world. If my kingdom were from this world, my followers would be fighting to keep me from being handed over. . . . But as it is, my kingdom is not from here" (John 18:36).

As the normalcy of civilization, the kingdom of Rome is grounded on, founded with, and protected by legionary violence. As the vision of post-civilization, the kingdom of God is nonviolent even—or especially—against its enemies, even—or especially to protect Jesus himself from execution (Q in Matt 5:45=Luke 6:35).

———·····••×××××××××✦×××××××××••·····———

This book's final two chapters focus on two sets of questions that are so interlocked together that their separation is mostly an artificial matter of balanced presentation. Chapter 10 concerns *why* questions and is dependent primarily on Paul's own letters. Chapter 11 concerns the consequent *what* questions, is dependent exclusively on Luke-Acts, and raises forcibly the distinction between fact and fiction, the separation of historical claim and apologetical function.

To start, then, the next Chapter 10 asks *why* did Paul travel to Jerusalem on what turned out to be his final visit? The answer involves an understanding of the transcendental importance for Paul of what we might call The Great Reconciliation Gift or, more simply, the Collection. It is what he himself called: first, "remembering the poor" (Gal 2:10); next, "the collection for the saints" (1 Cor 16:1); then, "the privilege of sharing (*koinonian*) in this ministry to the saints . . . the ministry to the saints . . . this ministry" (2 Cor 8:4; 9:1,12, 13); and finally, "I am going to Jerusalem in a ministry to the saints . . . the poor among the saints at Jerusalem . . . my ministry to Jerusalem . . . to the saints" (Rom 15:25,26,31).

Chapter 10 will also ask why that was all so profoundly important for Paul and why the Collection was not just for the Jerusalem "saints" in general but for "the poor among them" in particular.

Furthermore, if the Collection was transcendentally significant for Paul, was vital far beyond even alms or compassion, why is it absent completely from Luke-Acts? Was it unknown there or omitted there and if so, why?

Chapter 10

"IN THE TIME OF THE NOW"

The messianic event, which, for Paul, has already happened
with the resurrection . . . is present *en tō nyn kairō* [in the time of
the now] as the revocation of every worldly condition, released
from itself to allow for its use. . . . The word passes on to
the apostle, to the emissary of the Messiah, whose time is no
longer the future, but the present. That is why Paul's technical
term for the messianic event is *ho nyn kairos*, "the time of the
now"; this is why Paul is an apostle and not a prophet.

—Giorgio Agamben, *The Time that Remains*

We saw in Chapter 7 above that a relatively secure Pauline date is the
year 36 for his escape from Damascus and his first visit to Jerusalem.
That, however, gives us two other dependent ones: that first Jerusalem visit in 36 happened "three years" after his vocation-revelation
which, therefore, must have been in 33; and his second Jerusalem
visit happened "after fourteen years" (Gal 1:18; 2:1). But did that
mean "after fourteen years" from his vocation at Damascus in 33
or from his exfiltration from Damascus in 36? In other words, did
Paul's second Jerusalem visit and the Jerusalem Conference on male
convert-circumcision occur in 47 or 50—and why might that minor
chronological detail be important?[1]

Paul himself cites this reason for that second Jerusalem visit: "I
went up in response to a revelation" (Gal 2:2a) but he says nothing

---

[1] Many scholars whose work I respect and appreciate have worked out precisely dated chronologies for Paul's life and exactly argued sequences for his letters
but I am not convinced that we can establish such exact conclusions except partially here and there. In this book, therefore, 33, 36, and 47 CE are my only securely
precise dates with the Arabian Mission in the 30s, the Cypro-Anatolian Mission in
the 40s, and the Aegean Mission in the 50s.

about circumcision as the reason for rather than the subject of that visit. On the other hand, Luke-Acts records an occasion when,

> Prophets came down from Jerusalem to Antioch. One of them named Agabus stood up and predicted by the Spirit that there would be a severe famine over all the world; and this took place during the reign of Claudius. The disciples determined that according to their ability, each would send relief to the believers (*adelphois*) living in Judea; this they did, sending it to the elders by Barnabas and Saul. (Acts 11:27–30)

You might notice that, if the famine afflicted the whole world or even the whole Roman world, Antioch could have been as much in need as Jerusalem.

Josephus, however, records that once, when Jerusalem (and not the whole world!) "was hard pressed by famine," it was alleviated by grain from Egypt bought by the converted queen mother, Helena, and her son, Izates, of the small Parthian vassal state of Adiabene—in what is now northern Iraq (*JA* 20.51–53). Josephus later dates that famine-relief under the procurator Tiberius Julius Alexander in 46–48 (*JA* 20.101).

I conclude, therefore, that Paul's second Jerusalem visit was for famine relief from Antioch while Paul was still "under" Barnabas (Gal 2:1=Acts 11:27–30 & 15:1–2), and it should be dated to 47, that is "after fourteen years" from his vocation-revelation in 33. But why did something like famine relief require a causal "revelation" for Paul? Would not ordinary human compassion and/or communal fellowship have been enough to motivate "famine relief"—from Antioch to Jerusalem? At least for Paul, was something else involved over, under, around, and through that simple transmission of material assistance from Antioch to Jerusalem, something so transcendental that it required a "revelation," something that touched on the very integrity and continuity of this time of the now?

As we saw earlier in Chapter 7, Paul's rhetoric in describing that Conference visit, is polemcally disrespectful and truculently dismissive of the Jerusalem leadership—despite admitting that they agreed with his position (Gal 2:6–9). My conclusion is that Paul went to Jerusalem about famine relief as a reconciliation between Jerusalem and Antioch after the Cypro-Anatolian Mission but was ambushed theologically by "false believers secretly brought in, who slipped in to spy on the freedom we have in Christ Jesus, so that they might enslave us" (2:4). But who "brought them in secretly" except the leadership? No wonder Paul's language about "the leadership" was scathingly caustic!

As you also know from Chapter 7, the Conference resulted in a doomed compromise that established two Messianic/Christic missions—Peter's to Jews and Paul's to Gentiles—but with both necessarily operating in the same urban environments across the Roman Empire (Gal 2:7–9) Also, as already seen, the Sabbath-synagogue would be the primary focus and focal battleground—theological and political, social and economic—for both missions at the same time.

Finally, after that review of the fateful Jerusalem Conference, I focus on two Pauline comments, one at the start, the other at the end of his version of that bureaucratic compromise (*pace* Acts 15).

Immediately after citing that just-seen "revelation" as cause of his second Jerusalem visit, Paul continues with this: "I laid before them (though only in a private meeting with the seeming somebodies) the gospel that I proclaim among the Gentiles, in order to make sure that I was not running, or had not run, in vain" (Gal 2;2b). What did "running in vain" mean for Paul?

Had those seeming somebodies, James, Cephas, and John, demanded circumcision for male Messianic/Christics, Paul's revelatory vocation and apostolic mandate from God would not, could not, and should not have allowed him to agree that he was "running in vain." So what then did he mean by that phrase especially in light of his extreme rhetorical disrespect for those seeming somebodies?

Circumcision for Gentile male converts would have meant standard Jewish conversion procedures that simply negated the presence of the Messianic/Christic time of the now. Such an absolute split in vision, as distinct from a relative split in mission, would have meant that Paul—and those seeming somebodies too, for that matter—were all "running in vain." At transcendental stake for Paul was holding together the twin wings of Jewish and Gentile Messianic/Christics in and as the time of the now.

To do that, after the tactical split in mission (Gal 2:7–9), Paul concludes his account of the Jerusalem Conference with this: "James and Cephas and John . . . asked only one thing, that we remember the poor, which was actually what I was eager to do" (Gal 2:9,10).

Famine relief was, of course, an act of communal compassion but, because of its causal "revelation," it was also much more for Paul. For him it was only the first act in an ongoing attempt at reconciliation between Jewish and Gentile Messianic/Christics. That is the force of Paul's claim that he was actually eager to remember the poor—as a past, present, and future commitment. Maybe, just maybe, one vision might still perdure even after it split into two missions. At stake for Paul was whether the transcendental time of the now was already breaking apart into the trivial time of the now and then.

That ongoing reconciliation project between Jewish-born and Gentile-born Messianic/Christics involved for Paul a financial Collection from his Gentile converts in hopefully all four of his Roman mission-provinces: Galatia, Macedonia, Achaia, and Asia. During his Aegean Mission, the transcendental importance of that Reconciliation Collection is clear from the amount of time and energy, of planning and pleading, that Paul spent on it, as indicated in three different epistles.

Watch next that interface between Paul's Aegean Mission and Paul's Reconciliation Collection—a project so important for the integrity of the now-time that Paul consciously risked his life over it and eventually lost his life for it.

———·····◇·····———

In his first mention of this Collection project, Paul is writing to Corinth from Ephesus, capital of the Roman province of Asia. We know that from the final greeting in which, "the churches of Asia send greetings. Aquila and Prisca, together with the church in their house, greet you warmly in the Lord" (1 Cor 16:19). That second greeting presumes that Aquila and Prisc[ill]a, having moved from Corinth to Ephesus were, of course, known in that former city (Acts 18:2,18,19).

He says that, "I will stay in Ephesus until Pentecost," and that, "the churches of Asia send greetings" (1 Cor 16:8–9,19a). From Ephesus in Asia he sends to Corinth in Achaia both practical strategies and prudential tactics for its proper administration of the Collection:

> Concerning the collection for the saints: you should follow the directions I gave to the churches of Galatia.
> On the first day of every week, each of you is to put aside and save whatever extra you earn, so that collections need not be taken when I come.
> And when I arrive, I will send any whom you approve with letters to take your gift to Jerusalem.
> If it seems advisable that I should go also, they will accompany me. (1 Cor 16:1–4)

My presumption is that Paul set up that collection system with the Galatians as he returned through them on his westward journey to his Aegean Mission (Acts 16:1–5). The Collection project is not mentioned in the letter to the Galatians and it is a question whether or not it survived their bitter dispute over Paul's authority, identity, and integrity.

Also, to avoid even the possibility of financial impropriety, Paul would not gather or take the Collection himself. The Corinthians would select those to carry and administer their own gift to Jerusalem—with or without Paul.

Next, apart from fiscal plans about gathering the Collection, Paul also needed to make travel plans about delivering it. Either the Corinthians had presumed or Paul had promised them that he would come—directly?—from Ephesus to Corinth and sail from there with the assembled Collection to the Levantine coast and Jerusalem. But now an alternative Collection control and departure site appears on the horizon and the Corinthians are very displeased with Paul.

This is actually the crucial point behind Paul having to defend changes in his travel plans: who is to be in administrative charge of the Collection—Achaia or Macedonia?

Paul declares that he intended to visit Corinth not directly but indirectly, "after passing through Macedonia—for I intend to pass through Macedonia—and perhaps I will stay with you or even spend the winter, so that you may send me on my way, wherever I go" (1 Cor 16:5–6). But that doubled (and defensive?) mention of "passing through Macedonia" to get to Corinth reveals not just minor travel-plan changes but major competitive tension between Macedonia and Achaia about financial controls, administrative officers, and departure ports for the Jerusalem Collection. Again, later, Paul has to insist that, "I wanted to visit you on my way to Macedonia, and to come back to you from Macedonia and have you send me on to Judea" (2 Cor 1:16). Paul "wanted" to go first to Corinth but actually went first to Macedonia. For Corinth, that is not about Paul's minor travel changes but about Paul's major provincial priorities.

Remember, for what follows, that Paul wrote letters to both the Philippians and Thessalonians, that is, to two separate cities in Roman Macedonia, but only to the Corinthians, that is, to a single city in Roman Achaia. Which province did Paul prefer? Which province thought Paul should prefer it? Which province thought Paul did prefer it? (Statistics: Macedonia appears eleven times in four different letters; Macedonia and Achaia, three times in two different letters; Achaia, four times in two letters.)

In his second mention of this Collection project, Paul is again writing about it to the Corinthians but the change from casual serenity (1 Cor 16:1–4) to tortuous rhetoric (2 Cor 8–9) indicates that, between those letters, there occurred profound changes between Paul's relationship with his Corinthian supporters as well as in Paul's plans for both the gathering and delivering of the Collection.

Paul mentions his passage directly from Ephesus to Macedonia—rather than from Ephesus directly to Corinth—very defensively in 2 Cor 8:1–9:15. He dedicates two whole chapters on the Collection and speaks about Achaia's not-yet-fulfilled versus Macedonia's already-fulfilled collection. That involves, therefore, a change in control of the Collection's administration and port of departure—from

Achaia to Macedonia. In the process, he plies the Corinthians with a mini-masterpiece of rhetorical persuasion and psychological manipulation. (Some scholars see those two chapters as fragments of separate letters, by the way, but my focus here is on the content, whatever about the source, of 2 Cor 8–9.)

Although Paul had used Achaia's willingness for the project as an original incentive to encourage Macedonia (8:24; 9:2), the situation has now become reversed. Then, Achaia was the first to join the Collection project with a collection promise but now Macedonia is the first to complete it with a collection fulfillment. Hence that opening encomium for Macedonia to Corinth (8:1–5) sent, by the way, from Macedonia to Corinth! (2 Cor 2:12–13). With relations already tense between Paul and Corinth (2 Cor 2:1), he writes rather carefully but still quite firmly to inform them that the epicenter of the Collection is not Achaia but Macedonia and that its departure port will not be from Corinth but from Philippi's Neapolis. Watch these three steps.

First, since the Corinthians were resentful about his travel plans through Macedonia to Achaia (1 Cor 16:5), he claims that, at least originally, he had "wanted to visit you on my way to Macedonia, and to come back to you from Macedonia and have you send me on to Judea" (2 Cor 1:16). For the Collection, that would have given ascendancy to Achaia over Macedonia and a departure port from Corinth rather than, say, Neapolis.

Next, after general praise (8:7), he insists that he is advising and not commanding them, despite this: "now finish doing it, so that your eagerness may be matched by completing it" (8:8,11). He also shames them with this possibility that, "if some Macedonians come with me and find that you are not ready, we would be humiliated—to say nothing of you—in this undertaking" (9:4).

Finally, Macedonia, whose collection is ready to go, takes both administrative and executive control over Achaia, whose collection is still not assembled, by sending to them a newly but officially appointed three-person oversight committee for the project. Apart from individual administrative Collection carriers (1 Cor 16:3), there was now also an executive team of Collection controllers (2 Cor 8:16–24). Who were the three persons on that executive committee appointed by—Macedonia?

Titus was the chosen poster boy for the non-circumcision of male Gentile converts at the Jerusalem Conference (Gal 2:1,3). So, when Paul was encouraging Achaia "to remember the poor" in Jerusalem (Gal 2:10) and fulfill their collection-promise, Titus was the obvious companion to send to them (2 Cor 7:6,13,14; 8:6,16). But Titus was only one of a three-person executive team sent from Macedonia to Achaia: "As for Titus, he is my partner and coworker in your service; as for our brothers, they are messengers of the churches, the glory of Christ" (8:23). Why is Titus named but the other two team members are not named but identified only as "our brothers," Paul's standard but also very androcentric name for Messianic/Christics?

That omission is certainly not a dismissive put-down as "our brothers" are described with these high accolades—but notice the comment between them:

> *The Famous Brother.* "With him [Titus] we are sending the brother who is famous among all the churches for his proclaiming the good news; and not only that, but he has also been appointed by the churches to travel with us while we are administering this generous undertaking for the glory of the Lord himself and to show our goodwill."
>
> *The Executive Function.* "We intend that no one should blame us about this generous gift that we are administering, for we intend to do what is right not only in the Lord's sight but also in the sight of others."
>
> *The Eager Brother.* "With them we are sending our brother whom we have often tested and found eager in many matters, but who is now more eager than ever because of his great confidence in you." (8:18–22)

That middle section explains why, on this three-person team, Titus is praised, named, and clearly identified as "my partner and coworker in your service" (8:23). He is clearly identified as Paul's person while the other two members are praised but not named and thereby not identified as Paul's persons. It is as if he does not even know their names and therefore cannot control them as he might Titus.

What is at stake, of course, is to avoid not just the appearance but even the possibility that Paul could be accused of financial impropriety. (Does that mean, it had already happened?) It was better and safer, therefore, to the mind of the Macedonian churches, to appoint two overseers with Titus so that Paul could not possibly control the Collection by having Titus, a close companion, as its sole overseer. That is why, after those descriptions, Paul refers to them only as "the brothers" (2 Cor 8:23; 9:3,5). Also, of those two "brothers," the "famous" one is more important for Paul than the "eager" one. Later, the Famous Brother alone is mentioned along with Titus: "I urged Titus to go, and sent the brother with him" (2 Cor 12:18). I take leave of this Famous Brother for here and now but will return to him again in the next chapter.

In his final mention of this Collection project, Paul is writing to those not involved in it and he therefore says what he has never said before about its potential fate at Jerusalem—and about his own fate there as well.

As he ends his last epistle, Paul claims that he has "fully proclaimed the good news of Christ" around the eastern Roman Empire "from Jerusalem and as far around as Illyricum" (Rom 15:19)—which is inland and upland from the Adriatic coast of the Balkans. Now, however, with "no further place for [him] in these regions" (15:23), he is switching to the western Roman Empire. He plans to visit Rome on his way to "Spain" (15:24,28)—probably Tarraco/Tarragona immediately but maybe even Gādēs/Cádiz eventually. Then comes information that starts confidently but ends plaintively:

> At present, however, I am going to Jerusalem in a ministry to the saints; for Macedonia and Achaia have been pleased to share their resources with the poor among the saints at Jerusalem. . . . I appeal to you, brothers and sisters, by our Lord Jesus Christ and by the love of the Spirit, to join me in earnest prayer to God on my behalf, that I may be rescued from the unbelievers in Judea, and that my ministry to Jerusalem may be acceptable to the saints. (15:25–26,30–31)

(At the time of writing Romans, "Achaia" is, as in 1 and 2 Corinthians, still a hopeful part of the Collection-project.)

Paul recognizes that there is deadly danger for himself from non-Messianic/Christic Jews in Jerusalem. The only other time Paul speaks of personal "rescue" he repeats that term three time in the same verse: "God . . . who rescued us (with *hryomai*) from so deadly a peril will continue to rescue us (with *hryomai*); on him we have set our hope that he will rescue us (with *hryomai*) again" (2 Cor 1:10). Paul decides and accepts that this Reconciliation Collection requires his own personal presence and that it may cost him his life but is worth the risk of death.

Apart from final greetings in Romans, the last words from the historical Paul are that plea for prayer against "arrest" for himself and "non-acceptance" for the Collection at Jerusalem. He, of course, never got a chance to record what happened to the Collection or what happened to himself in Jerusalem or afterward. But that what pertains to the next Chapter 11.

——·· ··.·.:..:•:•:=•=*◇*•=:•:=•:.:.·.·:.··· ·——

Continuing with this chapter's *why*, I merge it now with a *who* by focusing on that phrase, "the poor among the saints at Jerusalem" (Rom 15:26) which specifies those recipients more exactly than simply as the "saints" (15:25,31). Also, more significantly, this links Paul's final mention of the "the poor" (*tous ptōchous*) at Jerusalem in Rom 15:26 back to that inaugural commitment to "remember the poor" (*tōn ptōchōn*) in Gal 2:10. And that, of course, raises this very basic question: who exactly are "the poor among the saints at Jerusalem" (Rom 15:26)?

Luke-Acts describes the inaugural Messianic/Christics in Jerusalem by claiming that, "all who believed were together and had all things in common; they would sell their possessions and goods and distribute the proceeds to all, as any had need" (Acts 2:44–45). Later, that theme of common property-for-all is repeated with the same phrase about distribution-to-need but also with more details:

> The whole group of those who believed were of one
> heart and soul, and no one claimed private ownership

of any possessions, but everything they owned was held in common . . . There was not a needy person among them, for as many as owned lands or houses sold them and brought the proceeds of what was sold. They laid it at the apostles' feet, and it was distributed to each as any had need. (4:32,34,35)

That general statement leads immediately into counterpointed positive and negative case-examples picking up that same phrase about the apostles' feet. First the positive: "Barnabas . . . sold a field that belonged to him, then brought the money, and laid it at the apostles' feet" (4:36–37). Then the negative: Ananias and Sapphira "kept back some of the proceeds, and brought only a part and laid it at the apostles' feet" as if it were the whole (5:1–11).

It is possible to consider those theme-linked and phase-linked passages as Luke-Acts' fictional idyll of communal perfection. But three points pull in the opposite—but qualified—direction.

First, there is that story about Ananias (5:1–6), even if Sapphira is a creative parallelism (5:7–11). It is pre-Lukan because it contradicts Luke's own claim that everyone gave all (4:32–35) by having Peter say to Ananias about his land: "While it remained unsold, did it not remain your own? And after it was sold, were not the proceeds at your disposal?" (5:4). That story is therefore pre-Lukan and makes no sense even as a cautionary fiction absent some degree of communal donation and communal distribution among those original Messianic/Christics in Jerusalem.

Second, from the wider Jewish matrix, think about those Essenes mentioned earlier in Chapter 3. Speaking of "Palestinian Syria" in his treatise *Every Good Man is Free*, Philo describes "certain persons, more than four thousand in number, called Essenes" (75)—a Jewish group to the radical left of religio-political options:

No one's house is his own . . . they dwell together in communities . . . have a common treasury and common disbursements; their clothes are held in common (*koinai*) and also their food is in common (*koinai*) . . . through public meals. All the wages which they earn in the day's

work they do not keep as their private property, but throw
them into the common (*koinēn*) stock . . . to be shared by
those who wish to use it. (85–86)

Josephus also describes "the Essenes" in both his *Jewish War* (2.119–161) and *Jewish Antiquities* (18.18–22). He agrees with Philo that, "they hold their possessions in common (*koina*) . . . and number more than four thousand" (18.20). But, in contrast to Philo, he divides the Essene movement into two classes.

The first class he describes in great detail (2.119–159) and notes not just that "their community of goods (*koinōnikon*) is truly admirable" (2.122) but that "marriage they disdain [and] they adopt other men's children" (2.120).

The second class gets a far shorter description (2.160–161) than that preceding one but the only difference that Josephus cites is that this second class does not practice celibate asceticism (2.160–161):

There is yet another order of Essenes, which while at
one with the rest in the mode of life, customs, and regu-
lations, differs from them in its views on marriage. They
think that those who decline to marry cut off the chief
function of life, the propagation of the race, and, what
is more, that, were all to adopt the same view, the whole
race would very quickly die out. (2.160)

Still, although those Essenes allow marriage, married intercourse must be practiced only for potential procreation. They have, for example, "no intercourse during pregnancy, thus showing that their motive in marrying is not self-indulgence but the procreation of children" (2.161).

Be that as it may, that distinction between two classes of Essenes is both supported, clarified, and more precisely differentiated by the discovery in the last two centuries of multiple copies of the rule book for each class.

In 1947, copies of the rule book for Josephus' first class of Essenes were discovered in a cave at Qumran among the so-called Dead Sea Scrolls, the sacred texts of a male group living lives of total common property and radical sexual asceticism in an adjacent ruined monastery. Along with fragmentary copies, the fullest text, from the first century BCE, is known today as the Community Rule (coded 1QS as the first Qumran cave's copy of the *Serekh haZahad* or *Rule of the Community*). In terms, for example, of entering the community, that Rule decreed that "if one is found among them who had lied knowingly concerning goods, he shall be excluded from the common table for a year and shall be sentenced to a quarter of his bread" (1QS 6.24–25). Communal suspension, however, is better than Ananias' divine execution.

In 1896, copies of the rule book for Josephus' second class of Essenes was discovered in the storeroom—or geniza— for worn out sacred texts of the Ben Ezra Synagogue in Egyptian Old Cairo. Along with fragmentary copies from the Qumran caves, the fullest Cairo copy is from twelfth century CE and known today as the *Damascus Document A*. It explicitly allows members to "beget children" (7.6–8) and decrees tithing for distribution to those in need rather than common property for all:

> This is the rule of the Many, to provide for all their needs: the salary of two days each month at least. They shall place it in the hands of the Inspector and the judges. From it they shall give to the orphans and with it they shall strengthen the hand of the needy and the poor, and to the elder who is dying, and to the vagabond, and to the prisoner of a foreign people, and to the girl who has no protector, and to the unmarried woman who has no suitor; and for all the works of the company. (14.1–17)

From all that new evidence about the Essenes, I imagine they had one ideal or model priests-led community that lived by total common property and radical sexual asceticism as well as many other groups that regulated property-sharing and marital intercourse. Turn back now, after that long excursus, from those early first-century Essenes (in Jerusalem?) to their contemporary early first-century Messianic/ Christics in Jerusalem.

Third, then, here is my proposal. I think that James had established in Jerusalem a group that lived by common property—whatever about sexual asceticism. They were not "the poor" as a group unwillingly deprived and economically impoverished. They were "The Poor" as a model group willingly living a share-life of common property, a life more encompassing than even regulated tithing for alms-giving. They were, therefore, "The Poor among the saints," that is, the Messianic/Christics, in Jerusalem (Rom 15:26).

Furthermore, I find that intuition confirmed, even if indirectly and obliquely, by the extreme personal status and individual prestige of James, both inside but especially outside those first Messianic/Christics in Jerusalem.

From inside, just compare the divergent versions of that Jerusalem Conference concerning James. Despite all other differences, James is very much in the ascendancy for Luke because, "After they finished speaking, James replied, 'My brothers, listen to me'" (Acts 15:13) but also for Paul with the priority of "James and Cephas and John" (Gal 2:9). He is also the fictional author of a New Testament letter—but, of course, Peter has two such letters.

From outside, Josephus tells a rather extraordinary story about the execution of James and especially about what happened because of it (*JA* 20.197–203). The scene was set in 62 CE when the procurator Festus was dead but the new procurator Albinus was still on the way from Rome. In that temporary interregnum the Sadducean high priest Ananus the Younger

> convened the judges of the Sanhedrin and brought before them a man named James, the brother of Jesus who was called the Christ and certain others. He accused them of having transgressed the law and delivered them to be stoned. Those of the inhabitants of the city who were considered the most fair-minded and who were strict (*akribeis*) in observance of the law were offended at this. (20.200–201)

They then protested both to the incoming Albinus, "who wrote to Ananus threatening to take vengeance upon him," and to King

Agrippa II, who "deposed Ananus from the high-priesthood" (20.203).

James, "the Lord's brother" (Gal 1:19), had remained and survived in Jerusalem for over thirty years after the crucifixion, even with Stephen stoned, James, the brother of John, executed, and Peter arrested (Acts 7:59; 12:2–3). I think it was his leadership of The Poor that made him a figure not of elected and official but of charismatic and ascetic authority both inside and outside The Saints in Jerusalem.

In summary. For Paul, the Collection was not about alms for the impoverished poor. If such had been intended, and it certainly was biblically mandated, those Gentile donors might well have wondered why not help our own poor first? Instead, that Collection was an attempt to hold together the two wings of a movement already in process of separation and disintegration. No matter how Paul might and did disagree with James, the subversive and powerful witness of his share-community was an ideal for Messianic/Christics everywhere just as the Essene ones were for Jews everywhere, and Qumran was for Essenes everywhere. For Paul, therefore, the Collection was profoundly grounded and deeply embedded in the time of the now and, indeed, in whether it was the transcendental time of the now or just another time of the now-and-then. For Paul, it held together the time and the now—as we see next in the conclusion of this chapter.

The Greek language has two very similar terms for time: *chronos* or *kairos*. *Chronos* or time-of-this-or-that, records the ordinary sequence determined now very evenly by atomic clocks but always very unevenly by human experience. *Kairos* or time-for-this-alone, records the disruptive event, the paradigm shift, the tradition swerve, the unexpected vision. (More ordinarily and simplistically: a wedding is a *kairos*, a marriage is a *chronos*—and, statistically, you know what *chronos* can do to that *kairos*.)

For example, Jesus' image of God's Rule, that is, of the Kingdom of God on Earth, as a mustard seed, is a parable of its temporality as *chronos*:

"What is the kingdom of God like? And to what should
I compare it? It is like a mustard seed that someone took
and sowed in his own garden; it grew and became a tree,
and the birds of the air made nests in its branches." (Mark
4:30–32; *Q* in Luke 13:18–19; Matt 13:31–32, as conflation of both)

But Jesus' image of God's Rule on earth as a pearl merchant, is a par-
adoxically contradictory parable of its temporality as *kairos*:

"The kingdom of heaven is like a merchant in search of
fine pearls; on finding one pearl of great value, he went
and sold all that he had and bought it." (Matt 13:45–46)

Think of that *kairos* as *chronos*: what does that merchant do next? Sell
it for advancement? Wear it for ornament? Hold it for admiration?
You see the problem: How do *kairos* and *chronos* interact? If *kairos* has
no *chronos*, what is its temporality? Is *kairos* the punctuation of *chronos'*
equilibrium?

As mentioned in this chapter's epigraph, Paul several times uses
a very special phrase difficult to translate, difficult to understand,
and, at least in Greek, somewhat redundant—presumably for emphasis. Paul wrote to the Romans about the *nyn kairos*, the "time of
the now" or the "now-time" (Rom 8:18) and of being *en tō nyn kairō*,
"in the time of the now," or "in now-time" (Rom 3:26; 11:5). Those
phrases are translated as "(in) the present time" (NRSV) and that is
rather feeble if you consider the equivalence created by this poetic
parallelism, with God speaking in Isa 49:8a:

At an acceptable time (*kairō dektō*) I have listened to you,
    and on a day of salvation I have helped you.
See, now is the acceptable time (*idou, nyn kairos euprosdektos*);
    see, now is the day of salvation! (2 Cor 6:2)

The *nyn kiros* or "now-time" is not just each, any, and every "present
time" but the time "acceptable" to God as "the day of salvation."

Only Paul uses that term *nyn kairos* in the New Testament and here is one final case of his fivefold usage:

> I do not mean that there should be relief for others and pressure on you, but it is a question of a fair balance between your present (*en tō nyn kairō*) abundance and their need, so that their abundance may be for your need, in order that there may be a fair balance. As it is written,[2] "The one who had much did not have too much, and the one who had little did not have too little." (2 Cor 8:13–15)

That Pauline text is, as you recall from earlier in this chapter, about the Collection but now construed as a "fair balance" or equal sharing between the financial abundance of the Gentiles and the spiritual abundance of the Jews.

Paul makes that same point to the Romans about the Collection: "if the Gentiles have come to share in their spiritual blessings, they ought also to be of service to them in material things" (15:27) but only in 2 Corinthians does he connect that reciprocity as something "in now-time." That association is a final clarification of why Paul would risk his life to deliver the Collection personally to Jerusalem. "Now-time" is the "day of salvation" for both Jews and Gentiles, that is for the whole world. For Paul, therefore, the Collection is the hope of that wholeness, the symbol of that universal salvation. The Collection was never a one-way process but always a mutuality, a reciprocity, an interactive cooperation, a "fair balance" between Jewish spiritual "abundance" and Gentile material "abundance."

Judaism's biblical tradition imagined a peaceful earth grounded in distributive justice, a world where "they shall beat their swords into plowshares, and their spears into pruning hooks; nation shall not

---

[2] That quotation is from Exod 16:18 LXX and refers to God's distributive justice of the manna in the desert during the Israelite exodus from Egypt (Exod 16:13–27); no matter how much each householder gathered, it turned out precisely enough for that household for that day. In other words, when God distributes food—or anything else?—the criterion of distributive justice is enough for that day —hence the Lord's Prayer's "daily bread" (*Q* in Matt 6:11=Luke 11:3). Enoughism is the criterion of creation.

lift up sword against nation, neither shall they learn war any more" (Mic 4:3b=Isa 2:4b). Also, of course, and as we noted earlier, that magnificent vision never imagined that a day would come, and now is, when the descendants of plowshares and pruning hooks would be civilization's equally pressing challenge.

Pharisaic Judaism's sectarian innovation imagined a final moment for that world when every single person who had ever lived would rise from the dead, be judged for what they had done, and be sanctioned for eternity in a heaven of reward or a hell of punishment. As an action of some God at end-time, that vision is still credible for many people but almost comically incredible for many—more?—as fear-mongering for financial profit. Still, if you bracket God and think instead of Evolution, it seems an accurate scenario for the future of our world in which everyone who has ever lived is responsible for the eventual fate of our world—individually and personally in small ways, universally and structurally in large ways.

Pharisaic Paul's Messianic/Christic revelation changed that end-time product into an in-time process—with the metaphor of a harvest started and its first fruits presented to God (1 Cor 15:12–13,16,20). Pharisaic faith was that, at least at end-time, the justice of God would be revealed in a finally and eternally justified world. But, said the Messianic/Christic Paul, that had already started in-time as now-time with the execution and resurrection of Jesus. His execution revealed a transcendental alternative to human wisdom. It disclosed a divine wisdom,

> not a wisdom of this age or of the rulers of this age, who are doomed to perish . . . [but] God's wisdom, secret and hidden, which God decreed before the ages for our glory. None of the rulers of this age understood this; for if they had, they would not have crucified the Lord of glory. (1 Cor 2:6–8)

For Paul, the Messianic/Christic Pharisee, the supreme religio-political horror of civilization's normalcy was that, "the God of this world" had not just killed "the glory of Christ, who is the image of

God" (2 Cor 4:4) but had executed him publicly, officially, and—legally. (Once again, then, for Paul, what boasting is left for human law?)

That archetypal tragedy had disclosed for Paul "the mystery that was kept secret for long ages" (Rom 16:25), namely, that, with civilization's official execution of the Messiah-Christ, universal resurrection, general judgment, and eternal sanctions had already begun in now-time. Put another way, the cosmic mystery is the revelation that, confronted with the challenge of transcendental nonviolence, the violent normalcy of civilization officially executes its embodiment.

Once again, and my apologies if I have said this too often, but whether you read that with or without God, whether you read it as a traditional theist, an impatient atheist, or an indifferent neither, think very seriously about Evolution and its challenge to us of universal responsibility, general accountability, along with heaven versus hell not as eternal sanctions in future life but as aboding options in present life, as the time of the now, now.

Chapter 11

"AND SO WE CAME TO ROME"

To be able to distinguish what is of true historical value and what is part of a hagiographic construction in Luke's text (to distinguish, for example, if the "cloven tongues of fire" mentioned in Acts 2:3 pertain to any historical event) is, without a doubt, a task beyond our present means.

—Giorgio Agamben, *The Time that Remains*

Throughout this book I have constantly and consistently chosen history with some apologetics in Paul's letters over apologetics with some history in Luke-Acts. As a smaller example, recall the Flight from Damascus in Paul's historically accurate anti-Nabatean version (2 Cor 11:31–33) versus Luke's polemically inaccurate anti-Jewish one (Acts 9:23–25); as a larger example, recall the historically impolite account of the disputes first at Jerusalem and then at Antioch in Paul's acerbic version (Gal 2:1–14) versus their conflation as a single apologetically polite conference in Luke-Acts' irenic version (Acts 15:1–29).

This book's final section has no such Pauline-Paul versus Lukan-Paul to allow due diligence on those competing sources. Instead, source discrimination can be established—with relative objectivity within our present means—between a pre-Lukan historical source and its Lukan apologetical redaction inside Acts 20–28 itself:

Table 3

Pre-Lukan Historical Source	*Lukan Apologetical Redaction*
16:10-17	20:1-4
20:5-15	20:16-38
21:1-18	21:19-26:32
27:1-28:16	28:17-31

Those four chunks of Lukan redaction in the right column encapsu-
late four chunks of pre-Lukan source in the left column. The rest of
this book is an argument for Table 3's interface of historical fact and
apologetical fiction—especially in Acts 20–28 for the end of Paul's
life. I begin with the pre-Lukan source because, to repeat, it contains
history with some apologetics while the Lukan redaction contains
apologetics with some history.

The Pre-Lukan Historical Source

(Table 3, left column). We saw already, in Chapter 7 above, how
Luke-Acts explained the inaugural Asia to Europe mission transition
as controlled by the Holy Spirit's drive westward from Jerusalem to
Rome (Acts 1:8; 13:2,4; 23:11). But that was a Lukan theological redaction and I turn now, as promised in Chapter 7, to how Paul himself understood that inaugural trans-Aegean voyage.

Scholars have identified, separated, and designated the four
units in Acts 16:10–17; 20:5–15; 21:1–18; and 27:1–28:16 as "we-
passages" because they involve the unexpected and unexplained
transition from the normal third-person authorial narrative with singular he/him or plural they/them to the first-person plural we/us
but never the singular I/me. And, of course, after a while the text
reverts back again from first to third person. It is precisely those four
we-passages that I designate here as a "pre-Lukan historical source"
(Table 3, left column).

In my best judgment, those we-passages were first composed
by an otherwise unknown travel-companion of Paul in the mid first
century and were used much later as a historical source by the equally
unknown author of Luke-Acts in the early second century.[1]

I look next at this four-passage pre-Lukan source under three
main subthemes: first, their Consecutive Unity; next, their Authorial
Profile; and finally, their Apologetical Purpose.

---

[1] That means, of course, that the companion of Paul named Luke—given
as fact in Philemon 24 and thence transposed as fiction to Col 4:14 and 2 Tim
4:11—is not the author of the we-passages nor, for that matter the author of what
we call Luke Acts.

Consecutive Unity

If you extract those four we-passages from their present redactional settings, what strikes you most forcibly is that you have primarily a maritime travel log with clear coastal way-sites and open-sea directions:

> [1] Acts 16:10–17: travel is from Troas in Asia, past the island of Samothrace, into the port of Neapolis in Macedonia, and thence inland to Philippi;
> [2] Acts 20:5–15: travel is from Philippi in Macedonia to Troas in Asia, on past Assos, Mitylene, Chios, and Samos, to Miletus;
> [3] Acts 21:1–18: travel is from Miletus, past Cos, Rhodes, Patara, and southern Cyprus, to Tyre, Ptolemais, Caesarea, and finally Jerusalem;
> [4] Acts 27:1–28:16: travel is from Caesarea Maritima, to Sidon, Myra, Cnidus, Crete, and shipwreck on Malta. Then from Malta past Syracus to Neapolitan Puteoli.

For a general matrix to that voyage, note that ships from Alexandria to Rome sailed against the dominant northwestern winds so that the smaller grain ships hugged the Mediterranean's eastern and northern coasts until finally they had to tack hard and often across the open sea and risk shipwreck on the southern coasts of Africa—or on an island like Malta. (For what follows: check internet maps.)

Paul's first ship was a cabotage from Adramyttium working its way back home from the Mediterranean's eastern to the Aegean's northeastern coast: from Caesarea, to Sidon, past the eastern "lee" of Cyprus and along the Cilician and Pamphylian coasts, to Myra, on todays' mid-southern Turkish coast. Since the ship was then turning northward to its home base, "we" left it there for one heading westward to Italy (27:1–5).

Paul's second ship was a typical grain ship (note "wheat" in 27:3), fighting head winds in transit from Alexandria towards Rome: from Cnidus, Cretan Salmone, Fair Havens, and Phoenix, to Cauda, and shipwreck on the island of Malta in mid-Mediterranean between today's Sicily and Tunisia (27:6–28:1).

Paul's third ship was another Alexandrian grain ship heading again for Rome: from Malta, past Sicilian Syracuse to port and Calabrian Rhegium to starboard, then through the Straits of Messina, and up the western coast of Italy to Puteoli, today's Pozzuoli, near Naples (28:11–13).

The first we-passage ends at Philippi (16:17) and the second one starts at Philippi (20:5–6). The second one ends at Miletus (20:15) and the third one starts at Miletus (21:1). But, after those two continuities, the final case is surprising: the third we-passage ends at Jerusalem (21:18) but the fourth one starts at Caesarea (27:1), with no Jerusalem to Caesarea connection and no explicit we-account of what happened in between those two cities. Was such data originally there but is now totally hidden within Lukan redaction? If so, why did Luke require such absorption precisely about the Collection's fate in Jerusalem? Hold that question in mind for later discussion.

This pre-Lukan we-source recounts what happened to Paul at Jerusalem only through a prophecy given before he gets there. A prophet named Agabus—introduced by Luke-Acts earlier in relation with the famine visit (11:28)—came down from Judea to Caesarea, "took Paul's belt, bound his own feet and hands with it, and said, 'the Jews in Jerusalem will bind the man who owns this belt and will hand him over to the Gentiles.'" Paul's response was that "I am ready not only to be bound but even to die in Jerusalem for the name of the Lord Jesus" (21:10–14).

The third we-passage ends with this hanging sentence: "When we arrived in Jerusalem, the brothers welcomed us warmly. The next day Paul went with us to visit James; and all the elders were present" (21:17–18). Without ever explaining what happened at and after that meeting, the pre-Lukan source ends abruptly as it is absorbed into the Lukan redaction and we/us cedes to he/him and they/them.

Authorial Profile

For Luke-Acts, as you recall from Chapter 7, it was a "Macedonian Man" (*anēr Makedōn*) who invited Paul in vision, apparition, and revelation to cross westward from Asia to Europe. For Paul, however, as I reconstruct the situation, it was an unnamed and unspecified Philippian patron, sponsor, and benefactor who invited Paul westward from Asia to Europe. My argument focuses on the first two of those four we-passages and on how the first one ends on a Troas-to-Philippi axis (16:11–12) while the second one starts with its reversal on a Philippi-to-Troas axis (20:5–6).

At Troas, Paul met a maritime trader from Philippi who was there presumably on business across the northern reaches of the Aegean Sea. He invited and sponsored Paul to leave Troas for Philippi—and therefore Asia for Europe—where he could probably act as his introductory patron. After the we-passage ends in 16:17, Paul's Macedonian patron stayed in his native city as Paul travelled southward through Athens to Corinth—as we saw in Chapter 7.

Later, therefore, the second we-passage starts at Philippi—where that first one had ended (Acts 16:17). In other words, Paul's Macedonian patron reunited with him in his hometown of Philippi and then accompanied him thereafter: "They went ahead and were waiting for us in Troas; but we sailed from Philippi after the days of Unleavened Bread, and in five days we joined them in Troas, where we stayed for seven days" (20:5–6).

Furthermore, I suggest that Paul's Philippian patron is the same individual still left unnamed but identified as the Famous Brother "appointed by the churches to travel with us while we are administering this generous undertaking" (2 Cor 8:18–19).

Paul names and praises very many of his companions and several of them—Aristarchus, Demas, Epaphroditus, Luke, Mark, Philemon, Prisca and Aquila, Timothy, Titus, Urbanus—are called "coworkers" (*synergoi*). Yet we have the Philippian patron/Famous Brother given no name, a splendid accolade, and the specific title of "traveling partner" (*synekdēmos*). The we-passages presume a traveling companion/partner for Paul and the Famous Brother is the only one officially accredited as such for this journey.

As the main Collection-executor travelling alongside Paul as Collection-minister, the Philippian patron would have had to write

up a report for the Macedonian churches on what happened to the
Collection as it moved from Troas to Jerusalem. Those we-passages
are now the Lukan-redacted remnant of the report of that one "appointed by the churches to travel" with Paul. Its importance for what
happened to the Collection at Jerusalem and to Paul from Jerusalem
to Rome was why it was preserved for over fifty years—maybe at
Philippi?—to be available much later as a heavily redacted source in
Luke-Acts.

Apologetical Purpose

In this fourth we-passage, Paul is travelling to Rome not for trial
as a suspect, not for appeal as an innocent, but for execution as a
condemned criminal: "When it was decided that we were to sail for
Italy, they transferred Paul and some other prisoners to a centuri-
on of the Augustan Cohort, named Julius" (28:1). Since they were
condemned criminals, for example, their guards were ready "to kill
the prisoners, so that none might swim away and escape" (27:42).

Granted that Paul travelled factually and historically for execution as a condemned criminal by Rome, how does the author
of the pre-Lukan historical we-source fictionally and apologetically give him vindication as an exculpated innocent—by God? That
transcendental exculpation is rhetorically accomplished by the even
balance between the pre-shipwreck events to Malta (27:13–44) versus the post-shipwreck events on Malta (28:1–10).

First, as prologue, is the shipwreck itself a total fiction invented
to prepare for what follows; could it be based, for example, on this
account in Josephus' autobiography?

> I reached Rome after being in great jeopardy at sea. For
> our ship foundered in the midst of the sea of Adria, and
> our company of some six hundred souls had to swim
> all that night. About daybreak, through God's good
> providence, we sighted a ship of Cyrene, and I and cer-
> tain others, about eighty in all . . . were taken on board.
> Landing safely at . . . Puteoli. (*Life* 5–6)

(Notice, by the way, that unlike the shift between they and we in a narrative, the shift between I and we in an autobiography is quite natural especially in recounting a ship voyage and especially a shipwreck. Imagine, today, calling for pick-up from a plane with, "we have just landed.")

There are certainly parallels between the shipwrecks of Josephus and Paul: both cite the same general locality, "the sea of Adria" (27:27) which then extended south of our Adriatic Sea; both number the on-board passengers (27:37); both mention swimming to safety (27:43); and both specify "daybreak" (27:33). Still, that pre-Lukan we-source has an almost obsessive-compulsive attention to maritime detail as if he were filling out a captain's log—to the bitter end (pun intended). I prefer, therefore, to take the shipwreck to Malta as historical fact but against the ancient understanding of what such a disaster entailed.

Think, for example, of that brilliantly satirical and powerfully subversive story about the recalcitrant prophet Jonah who, told by God to go eastward by land, goes disobediently westward by sea. In response, "the Lord hurled a great wind upon the sea, and such a mighty storm came upon the sea that the ship threatened to break up" (Jonah 1:4). In ancient maritime culture, a shipwreck meant that the fates or the gods were claiming the life of some criminal on board. To save the ship and all on board, it was imperative to identify and remove that object of divine retribution, and so, "they picked Jonah up and threw him into the sea; and the sea ceased from its raging" (Jonah 1:15).

In the present case of Luke-Acts' shipwreck on Malta, however, "we were in all two hundred seventy-six persons in the ship" and "all were brought safely to land" (27:37,44). In other words, although the shipwreck was caused by divine retribution against someone on board, all escaped to land, and so the miscreant was not identified—and any onward ship would again be in danger. This allows the pre-Lukan we-source to turn from fact to fiction, from history to apologetics, and to continue its divine certification of Paul's innocence:

> Paul had gathered a bundle of brushwood and was putting it on the fire, when a viper, driven out by the heat,

fastened itself on his hand. When the natives saw the
creature hanging from his hand, they said to one another,
"This man must be a murderer; though he has escaped
from the sea, justice has not allowed him to live." He,
however, shook off the creature into the fire and suffered
no harm. (28:3–5)

Next, Paul heals a member of Malta's leading family and "the rest
of the people on the island who had diseases also came and were
cured" (28:9). Paul's redemptive activity on land continues and con-
summates that at sea where his advice had always been prescient-
ly correct (27:9,21) and his assistance always successfully salvific
(27:31,36). Once again, that continues divine verification of Paul's
innocence—by God, *pace* Rome.

Finally, when they depart Malta, they are well provisioned by
the grateful Maltese, (28:10), they sail under the protection of Castor
and Pollux, twin half-brother patrons of honest sailors (28:11), and
they find a good south wind to take them safely through the dangerous Straits of Messina northward towards Naples (28:13). Paul may
be completely inculpated by Rome but he is completely exculpated by
God.

The hearer/reader almost forgets completely that, no matter
how innocent he is before God, Paul is still travelling to his execution
at Rome. In Paul's own words: "Last night there stood by me an angel
of the God to whom I belong and whom I worship, and he said, 'Do
not be afraid, Paul; you must stand before the emperor; and indeed,
God has granted safety to all those who are sailing with you'" (Acts
27:23–24).

The Lukan Apologetical Redaction

The Lukan apologetical redaction in Acts 20-28 (Table 3, right column) brings to a powerful combination and climactic presentation
those three major constitutive themes proposed earlier within the
generative vision of Luke-Acts: first, Internal Messianic/Christic
Harmony; second, External Jewish Turmoil; and third, Official Roman Exculpation. I look at each of those themes separately but, of

course, each theme supports the other and the last circles back to the first.

First: Internal Messianic/Christic Harmony. This theme of harmony, peace, and order within the Messianic/Christic community focuses on Paul through three speeches placed on his lips by Luke-Acts: one is to his Messianic/Christic followers at Miletus (20:18–35), another is to his non-Messianic/Christic fellow Jews at Jerusalem (22:6–21), and a final one is to the highest local Gentiles, the governing Roman authorities, at Caesarea Maritima (26:12–18). We saw before that, as an educated rhetorician, the author of Luke-Acts knows how to invent speech-in-history, create speech-in-context, and compose speech-in-character. Educated readers then—and now?—would know to expect and appreciate the authorial purposes and apologetical intention of all such creative exercises.

At Miletus, Luke-Acts creates a farewell *apologia pro vita sua* from Paul to the elders of the church at Ephesus (Acts 20:18–35). You can see rather clearly how he inserts it into the originally continuously ongoing second-to-third we-passage past Miletus (20:15) towards Rhodes (21:1). As the ship sailed southward along the eastern Aegean coastline in the pre-Lukan we-source, Miletus was mentioned but Ephesus was not. Therefore, for the Lukan recension to create this speech to those Ephesian elders, they had, perforce, to come to Miletus. That is one place where we can see a clear interface between pre-Lukan source and Lukan redaction as the latter adjusts the former to its purpose.

Paul's Miletus speech is in the tradition of both Greco-Roman and biblical farewells but reflects especially their classical archetype in Plato's farewell speech for Socrates. There, however, it precedes not just the ordinary death but the official execution of Socrates (*Phaedo* 115b–118). So also with Luke's farewell speech for Paul who says that he is on his "way to Jerusalem" for "imprisonment and persecutions" but that "I do not count my life of any value to myself" (20:22–24; see also 21:4,10–14).

The speech opens on the first defensive themes of Internal Messianic/Christic Harmony but combines it with a gesture towards the second one of External Jewish Turmoil: "You yourselves know how I lived among you the entire time from the first day that I set foot in Asia, serving the Lord with all humility and with tears, enduring the trials that came to me through the plots of the Jews" (20:18–19).

Then, as expected from its creation by Luke-Acts, Paul's mission has been "to both Jews and Greeks" and not exclusively to Greeks/Gentiles—despite that as the focus both mandated by God and agreed upon at Jerusalem (Gal 1:16; 2:7–9).

Furthermore, the farewell address delivers a self-defense from Paul: "I am not responsible for the blood of any of you. . . . I coveted no one's silver or gold or clothing" (20:26, 33). Also, and maybe even more significantly, this Lukan-Paul warns that, "Some even from your own group will come distorting the truth in order to entice the disciples to follow them" (20:30).

After his Miletus speech offers a defensive address to this internal group—Paul's own followers and supporters—his last two speeches are to external groups and are, as already-seen, variations on Paul's vocation-revelation. We can understand, however, why Luke-Acts wants them precisely in this section as final defensive addresses first to Jewish authority (22:6–21) and then to Roman power (26:12–18).

Second: External Jewish Turmoil. The repeated theme of riotous and murderous "Jews," invented inaugurally and archetypally by Luke-Acts for Jesus at Nazareth (Luke 4:29), is consummated here with Paul at Jerusalem (21:9–26:32).

As a first aspect of such Jewish turmoil, Paul's initial accusers are "some Jews from Asia," who fail even to follow up with an appearance before the Roman tribunal (21:27; 24:19). Those who do appear are Jerusalem Jews who accuse Paul of crimes they cannot "prove" (24:13; 25:7). Besides, those were Jewish crimes that Roman power "did not expect" (25:19). They are Jewish accusations that Paul "has actually brought Greeks into the temple and has defiled this holy place" (21:28); and that "he even tried to profane the temple, and so we seized him" (24:6).

As a second aspect of such Jewish turmoil, Paul's accusers were already covertly acting outside the Roman law which they were overtly using: "they were trying to kill him" (21:31); "tear Paul to pieces" (23:10); "the Jews joined in a conspiracy and bound themselves by an oath neither to eat nor drink until they had killed Paul" (23:12); and "were, in fact, planning an ambush to kill him" (25:3).

Furthermore, later, Luke-Acts contrasts those Jerusalem Jews with the Romans Jews who tell Paul that, "We have received no letters from Judea about you, and none of the brothers coming here has reported or spoken anything evil about you" (28:21).

Third: Official Roman Exculpation. As a first aspect of this theme, the two-volume Gospel according to Luke-Acts now comes to a soaring crescendo with official declarations of innocence for Paul at the end of the latter volume that transcend even those for Jesus at the end of the former one.

At the end of volume 1 of Luke-Acts, Jesus is declared innocent of any crime by all three major levels of Roman power and imperial authority:

> Military Officer: by that unnamed "centurion" beneath the cross who said that "Certainly this man was innocent." (Luke 23:47)
>
> Client Ruler: by Prince Herod Antipas "who treated him with contempt . . . and sent him back to Pilate." (Luke 23:11)
>
> Roman Official: by Pontius Pilate, ruler over part of the Jewish homeland, who said that "I find no basis for an accusation against this man . . . I have not found this man guilty of any of your charges. . . . A third time . . . I have found in him no ground for the sentence of death." (Luke 23:4,14,22)

Then, correspondingly, at the end of volume 2 of Luke-Acts, Paul is declared innocent by even higher representatives of those same three major levels of Roman power and imperial authority:

> Military Officer: by the tribune Claudius Lysias who wrote that "I found that he was accused concerning questions of their law, but was charged with nothing deserving death or imprisonment." (Acts 23:29)

Client Ruler: by King Herod Agrippa II, "The king . . .
the governor and Bernice . . . said to one another, 'This
man is doing nothing to deserve death or imprisonment.'
Agrippa said to Festus, 'this man could have been set free
if he had not appealed to the emperor.'" (Acts 26:30–32)

Roman Official: by Porcius Festus, ruler over all of the
Jewish homeland, who said that Paul's "'accusers . . . had
certain points of disagreement with him about their own
religion. . . . But I found that he had done nothing deserv-
ing death.'" (Acts 25:18–19,25)

You will notice how Luke-Acts repeats its apologetical mantra on
Roman official lips: accusations against the Messianic/Christics are
about Jewish law and of no concern to Roman law: so from Gallio
at Corinth (18:15) through Claudius Lysias at Jerusalem (23:29) to
Porcius Festus at Caesarea (25:18–19,25).

As a second aspect of this exculpation theme, Luke-Acts must
still explain why this all-innocent Paul is travelling to Rome as a prisoner under guard. The Lukan solution is to negate Paul's standing as
a guilty criminal condemned to imperial execution and portray him
instead as an endangered innocent seeking imperial vindication. That
absolution requires two steps.

In the first step, Paul claims to be a Roman citizen. Furthermore, unlike the tribune Claudius Lysias, Paul did not acquire that
status later in life but was born with it—the Lukan-Paul is a freeborn
Roman citizen (22:25–29).

There was also an earlier such claim of Roman citizenship at
Philippi that involved both Paul and Silas. As we saw earlier, this
basic story is part of Luke-Acts' hierarchical parallelism of events
that happened first to Peter and then to Paul. In this example, Peter
(5:17–26) and Paul (16:25–39) have miraculous escapes from prison.
Paul and Silas are "beaten with rods" (16:23—not "severely flogged"
as in NRSV). What is unlikely in the Lukan account, however, is that
Paul does not claim that he and Silas are "Roman citizens" before-
hand to prevent that beating but only afterward to obtain an apology
for it (16:7–38). If prevention had happened, of course, Luke's whole
narrative could not have proceeded!

As it is, the Lukan-Paul, the "Roman citizen" beaten and imprisoned by an ultimately sympathetic official at Philippi, is an early distant preparation for Paul, the "Roman citizen," not beaten and not imprisoned by an ultimately sympathetic official at Jerusalem.

There is, however, nothing anywhere in Paul's own letters that even hints at his being a "Roman citizen." In fact, his own autobiographical data distinguished between two types of bodily punishment: "Five times I have received from the Jews the forty lashes minus one. Three times I was beaten with rods (*errabdisthēn*)" in 2 Cor 11:24–25. That distinguishes between Jewish and Roman beatings and Paul uses the same verb there as Luke-Acts did when Paul and Silas were "beaten with rods (*hrabdizein*)" at Philippi in (16:22). In my own best judgment, therefore, Paul was not a Roman citizen—freed or freeborn—but Luke-Acts needed that status to strengthen this next step.

In the second step, Paul "appeals" to the imperial tribunal and is only sent to Rome at his own demand. Luke-Acts then beats that "appeal" like a drum (25:10,11,12,21,25; 26: 32; 28:19).

Around the year 60, Felix, the Roman governor of Judea retired, Festus, the new governor took office (24:27), and Paul appeared before him. When he said that, "'I have in no way committed an offense against the law of the Jews, or against the temple, or against the emperor'" (25:8), Festus "wishing to do the Jews a favor, asked Paul, 'Do you wish to go up to Jerusalem and be tried there on these charges before me (*ep' emou*)?'" (25:8–9; the Greek text ends with before me).

As an innocent Roman citizen accused by the Jews on Jewish matters, any such person should have accepted judgment in Jerusalem but "before me," that is, before the Roman governor Festus. Whatever about fear of assassination, Paul (allegedly) had a protective escort of 470 soldiers from Jerusalem to Caesarea (23:23–24) and, presumably, would have similar protection back to Jerusalem. Instead, we get the first instance of the chant-like repetition of "appeal" to Rome:

> I am appealing to the emperor's tribunal; this is where
> I should be tried. I have done no wrong to the Jews, as

you very well know. Now if I am in the wrong and have
committed something for which I deserve to die, I am
not trying to escape death; but if there is nothing to their
charges against me, no one can turn me over to them. I
appeal to the emperor. Then Festus, after he had con-
ferred with his council, replied, "You have appealed to
the emperor; to the emperor you will go." (25:10–12)

Paul's "appeal" is so important for Luke-Acts that he has Festus repeat it when the Jewish Herodian King Agrippa II and his widowed
sister Bernice "arrived at Caesarea to welcome Festus" (25:13):

When the accusers stood up, they did not charge him
with any of the crimes that I was expecting. Instead they
had certain points of disagreement with him about their
own religion and about a certain Jesus, who had died, but
whom Paul asserted to be alive. Since I was at a loss how
to investigate these questions, I asked whether he wished
to go to Jerusalem and be tried there on these charges.
But when Paul had appealed to be kept in custody for the
decision of his Imperial Majesty (*tou Sebastou*), I ordered
him to be held until I could send him to the emperor.
(25:19–21)

Notice that, this time, "to Jerusalem and be tried on these charges" in
25:20 does not end with "before me" as in 25:9. Unless you are reading very carefully, Luke-Acts makes it seem that Paul's only choice
was between a Jewish trial at Jerusalem with assassination likely and
an Imperial trial at Rome with exculpation likely. Instead, there could
also have been a Roman trial at Jerusalem before Festus. In other-
words, for Luke-Acts, Paul had to "appeal" to Rome for supreme
and ultimate vindication because Jerusalem was already a murderous
venue (23:12–15).

In any case, Luke-Acts continues that insistence that Paul was
only sent to Rome because he himself had "appealed" to go there.
Paul's own defense-speech—that third and final version of his Damascus experience—is bracketed with assertions of his innocence as

well as why, granted innocence, he was going to Rome under guard. Before Paul speaks there is this official and public ("all here present") statement:

> Festus said, "King Agrippa and all here present with us, you see this man about whom the whole Jewish community petitioned me, both in Jerusalem and here, shouting that he ought not to live any longer. But I found that he had done nothing deserving death; and when he appealed to his Imperial Majesty, I decided to send him." (25:24–25)

Then, after Paul finished his defense, there was another official and public ("those who had been seated with them") declaration of Paul's innocence accompanied again by his own "appeal" to Rome:

> The king got up, and with him the governor and Bernice and those who had been seated with them; and as they were leaving, they said to one another, "This man is doing nothing to deserve death or imprisonment." Agrippa said to Festus, "This man could have been set free if he had not appealed to the emperor." (26:30–32)

Luke-Acts' usual apologetical defense rings out explicitly: any turmoil around Paul is all about disagreements over Jewish law and not about crimes against Roman law. But, in the Lukan redaction, all those apologetical assertions mean that Paul travels to Rome not for execution as a condemned criminal, not even for trial as an indicted one, but for imperial exculpation as an innocent Roman citizen accused only about Jewish matters by murderous fellow Jews.

For the record, no Roman official mindful of his job and career would create the anomaly and incur the expense of sending an already completely exculpated prisoner under guard to Rome. For what reason? Under what excuse? With what accusation or indictment?

———·····✦·····———

In any case, as seen so far, both the pre-Lukan source and the Lukan recension, agree that Paul is innocent. The difference is that the source sends Paul to Rome as a convicted criminal who is exculpated by God after departure while the recension sends him there as an unconvicted innocent who is exculpated by Rome before departure. In both cases, however, there is one glaring omission in and one very obvious question about Luke-Acts.

For Paul, from Chapter 10, the Reconciliation-Collection was of transcendental importance. His own foundational vision of the universalism of Jews-and-Gentiles was not based on some Greek post-Alexander cultural universalism or some Roman post-Augustus imperial universalism. Pauline universalism was founded and grounded on resurrection! What could be more absolutely universal than the resurrection-judgment-sanction of all the dead from his Pharisaic past or its already ongoing "first fruits" with Jesus from his Messianic/Christic present?

In the light of that Pauline vision comes this Lukan question: Why is there nothing in Luke-Acts about that Reconciliation-Collection? Does it not know about the Collection or, rather, does it know about the Collection and deliberately negate it? And, if so, why so? Finally, does any negation still leave traces that let us answer that why?

Come back, one last time, to that (in)famous Jerusalem Conference, in its orderly peaceful, procedurally correct, communally harmonious, but apologetically fictional Lukan version in Acts 15:1–29—versus its historically bitter Pauline version in Gal 2:1–14. But always retain in mind the difference between a split in theological vision and a split in tactical mission.

Luke-Acts completely negates any split in vision and, therefore, in mission. But, for Paul, while a split-mission is tactically tolerable with "James and Cephas and John" on mission to Jews but "Barnabas and me" on mission to Gentiles (Gal 2:9), a split-vision breaches resurrection's universalism and would be catastrophic to the time-as-now. The Collection from Paul's Gentile communities to James' model Poor community is the last best hope of avoiding that catastrophe (Gal 2:10; Rom 15:26).

The version of the Jerusalem Conference in Acts 15 suppresses mention of any split-in-mission let alone any split-in-vision within the Messianic/Christic community. There could be and would be no Lukan Collection to reconcile separate wings of missionary activity because such could not and did not ever happen at that serenely pacific Jerusalem Conference in Luke-Acts.

Despite that overall elimination of the Collection by Luke-Acts, there are two moments—one at the departure and another at the arrival of the Collection—which reveal that Luke-Acts knows all about it but deliberately avoids mentioning it.

Paul's Departure with the Collection

Luke-Acts locates Paul in Macedonia ready to sail from Philippi, actually Neapolis, and "He was accompanied by Sopater son of Pyrrhus from Beroea, by Aristarchus and Secundus from Thessalonica, by Gaius from Derbe, and by Timothy, as well as by Tychicus and Trophimus from Asia" (20:4). Those individuals are from three of Paul's four Roman provinces: Macedonia is represented by Sopater, Aristarchus, and Secundus; Galatia is represented by Gaius and Timothy; and Asia is represented by Tychicus and Trophimus.

Those are the community-appointed Collection-carriers (1 Cor 16:3). But where is Titus and where are the Collection-carriers from Paul's fourth province of Achaia? Did the Corinthians refuse Titus and fail Paul? When Paul cited "Macedonia and Achaia" (Rom 15:26) as Collection-contributors was that still possibility and not yet—or never—actuality? In any case, and whatever about Corinth, Luke-Acts knows about the Collection but prefers to avoid mentioning it by focusing on the names and origins rather than the purposes and functions of those traveling with it to Jerusalem alongside Paul.

Paul's Arrival with the Collection

Luke-Acts gives two glimpses of what actually happened directly to the Collection and indirectly to Paul because of it in Jerusalem. Also, what Luke-Acts lets us see is correlated precisely with Paul's twin fears of what might happen there to both it and himself (Rom 15:30–31).

First, Paul had asked his Roman hearers/readers for prayers "that my ministry to Jerusalem may be acceptable to the saints" (Rom 15:31b).

As seen already, Luke-Acts ends the third unit of its we-source with this: "When we arrived in Jerusalem, the brothers welcomed us warmly. The next day Paul went with us to visit James; and all the elders were present" (Acts 21:17–18). So far, so good. But then James says "many thousands of believers . . . among the Jews . . . all zealous for the law . . . have been told about you that you teach all the Jews living among the Gentiles to forsake Moses, and that you tell them not to circumcise their children or observe the customs" (21:20–21). That was not, of course, Paul's message but an easy—if invidious and hostile—conclusion from it. In any case, James' solution is that,

> We have four men who are under a vow. Join these men,
> go through the rite of purification with them, and pay for
> the shaving of their heads. Thus all will know that there
> is nothing in what they have been told about you, but that
> you yourself observe and guard the law. (21:23b–24)

Luke-Acts completes James' demand with a recitation of the four-fold prohibition for Gentiles in close living-association with Jews—no idols, no blood, no strangled meat, no fornication. That, however, was fictionally quoted by James in Acts 15:20 and 15:29a and is now repeated fully from him here in 21:25.

However, therefore, James actually formulated his demand, and whatever in-Temple ritual it actually involved, I think some payment involving not just Paul himself—for whose personal acceptance of ritual head-shaving Acts 18:18 had already prepared us—but others from the Poor, was the condition for James accepting the Collection. Presented with Paul's Reconciliation-Collection, James did not refuse it directly but accepted it only indirectly. The Collection was "acceptable to the saints" but only as used by Paul for them and not as taken from Paul by them.

Second, Paul had also asked his Roman hearers/readers for prayers "that I may be rescued from the unbelievers in Judea" (Rom 15:31a).

As I understand Paul, he would not have had any problem with using part or all of the Collection for the purpose suggested by James. But having arrived in Jerusalem with a group of Gentiles and then going into the inner Temple with a group of Jews, a deadly accusation was possible, plausible, and maybe even inevitable.

Historically speaking, there was nothing against non-Jews being in the Temple—for whom else was Herod's great Court of the Gentiles intended! But, as the Greek signs on the balustrade between that Court of the Gentiles and the Court of the Jews warned: "no foreigner is to enter within the balustrade. . . . Whoever is caught will be himself responsible for his ensuing death" (Archaeological Museum, Istanbul). Despite the Lukan escalation of Gentile interdiction to the whole Temple rather than just to its Inner Court, I accept the basic historical truth of that accusation.

I therefore consider that the accusation of having brought Gentiles across the boundaries marked out by those lethal warnings is probably as close as we can ever get to what actually happened to Paul on that fatal visit to Jerusalem.

—·····◆·····—

My final point compares those just-seen accounts, one in pre-Lukan source and the other in Lukan redaction, of what happened to Paul and, since both agree that he went to Rome under guard, what crime should we plausibly imagine when a source retains too little and a redaction invents too much about it? Despite or because of their apologetical exculpation, be it from God or Rome, of what crime might Paul have plausibly been convicted in Jerusalem that would have had him sent under guard to Rome?

On the one hand, if that pre-Lukan source in those we-passages were all that existed (Table 3, left column), we would think that Paul was traveling to Rome for execution as a condemned criminal. The conclusion then would be that—on the way there—Paul had to be proved guiltless by God since he would be executed as guilty by Rome. In other words that source's last sentence, "When we came into Rome, Paul was allowed to live by himself, with the soldier who was guarding him" (28:16), would make a reader presume that it had simply omitted the concluding phrase: until he was executed.

On the other hand, if that Lukan redaction were all that existed (Table 3, right column), we would know the exact opposite. We would think that Paul was travelling to Rome having been declared innocent not by God but by every level of Roman authority; that Paul had demanded to go there on appeal for final and supreme imperial exculpation; that Paul was almost under protective custody against potential Judean-Jewish assassination. In other words, that redaction's last sentence, "He lived there two whole years at his own expense and welcomed all who came to him, proclaiming the kingdom of God and teaching about the Lord Jesus Christ with all boldness and without hindrance" (28:30–31), would make a reader presume that it had simply omitted the concluding phrase: until he was exculpated.

Granted that divergence between pre-Lukan we-source and Lukan redaction, what is the most likely crime Paul committed in Jerusalem that would have sent him for execution—and not exculpation—to Rome?

In answer, I begin with the precedents of Roman civil law as assembled and organized in the 200s CE by the celebrated jurist Julius Paulus, who was nicknamed Prudentissimus, and was the first to argue that the accused was innocent until proven guilty since the burden of proof is with *"qui dicit, non qui negat."* In Title XXII: Concerning Seditious Persons, his first precedent was that: "The authors of sedition and tumult, or those who stir up the people, shall, according to their rank, either be crucified, thrown to wild beasts, or deported to an island" (*The Opinions of Julius Paulus Addressed to His Son*, 5.22.1; available online).

Think about three Messianic/Christics who were condemned for nonviolent activism, that is, for sedition, tumult, and stirring up the people: Jesus of Nazareth was sent to a cross, Ignatius of Antioch was sent to an arena, and John of Revelation was sent to an island. Think especially of the obvious parallel between the case of Paul who travelled to Rome by sea along with other prisoners in the late 50s (27:1,42) and Ignatius who travelled there by land, also with other prisoners, in the early 100s.

In transit to a Roman execution, Ignatius wrote letters from Smyrna to Ephesus, Magnesia, Tralles, and Rome; then from Troas to Philadelphia, Smyrna, and Polycarp, bishop of Smyrna. But notice what is missing: he never wrote a letter back to his home community at Antioch nor asked any other community he visited or addressed to do so for him. Also, he wrote *To the Philippians* that, "it was reported to me that the Church which is in Antioch in Syria is in peace" (10.1), and *To Polycarp* that, "the Church which is in Antioch has peace through your prayers" (7.10).

Along with other scholars, I think that "peace" was restored at Antioch not just after but because Ignatius was gone. Strife involving ideology and personality, strife both inside the Messianic/Christic community itself and outside it with its non-Messianic/Christic Jewish neighbors, must have spilled out into the streets as civic turmoil and urban unrest. For that, Ignatius was held responsible, condemned to death, and, with groups for and against him, the wisest procedure was to send him to Rome for execution—out of sight at Antioch, out of mind at Antioch.

My best reconstruction is that, as with Ignatius at Antioch, so with Paul at Jerusalem. Leaving aside Luke-Acts' perfect storm of Roman exculpation as apologetical fiction, I think that Paul's arrival created turmoil, stirred up strife, and created enough civic unrest that the solution was to condemn Paul but send him far away to Rome for execution. My conclusion is that Paul went on his way to Rome not for trial but for death, not for vindication in the imperial court but for execution in the imperial arena.

Paul, *pace* Luke, was not a Roman citizen who was executed with the "privilege" of beheading by the sword. Instead, he died among others in a Roman arena; and those among whom he died were probably not Messianic/Christics, but were, like the "prisoners" who accompanied him from Caesarea to Rome (Acts 27:1,42), a group of both Jews and Gentiles, united together at least in death.

When, today, you stand in Rome before the great basilicas of St. Peter's in the Vatican or St Paul's Outside the Walls, the statue of Paul holds a prominent sword in his right hand. That is the fictional legacy of the Lukan-Paul. Still, those same two Roman statues show a scroll or codex in Paul's left hand. That is the factual legacy of the Pauline-Paul. But is that legacy relevant in now-time or, better, as now-time?

In Conclusion

The Latin image on the second unnumbered page of this book says: "Paul gives letters to his disciples Timothy and Silas to be taken through the whole world (*per universum orbem*)." For Paul himself, his empowering vision was for "the whole world" across all-time and all-space, so what of that claim of permanent relevance now?

First, Judaism's biblical tradition imagined a some-day peaceful earth grounded in distributive justice, a world where, to repeat one final time, "they shall beat their swords into plowshares, and their spears into pruning hooks; nation shall not lift up sword against nation, neither shall they learn war any more" (Mic 4:3b=Isa 2:4b). Also, of course, and as we noted earlier, that soaring vision never imagined that a day would come, and now is, when plowshares and pruning hooks would themselves become civilization's equally pressing challenge. *Homo sapiens* has launched not a one-front but a three-front onslaught—on itself, all other species, and the world itself as environment.

Next, over against the cross-cultural vision of divine justice by Individual Ascension for certain privileged persons like a Romulus or a Moses, Pharisaic Judaism's sectarian innovation imagined divine justice by Universal Resurrection for the whole human race through cosmic responsibility and ultimate accountability. There would be, there had to be, a final reckoning for "this world" when every single person who had ever lived would rise up together, would be judged for what each had done, and would be sanctioned for eternity in a heaven of reward or a hell of punishment. Otherwise, where is divine justice in an unjust world? Otherwise, when is divine justice in an unjust world?

That vision is still credible for many people as the action of God at end-time. But, maybe for many more, it is credible only as religious terrorism or theological fanaticism. Still, if you bracket the Big God and think instead of the Big Bang, it seems an accurate scenario for the future of our world in which everyone who has ever lived is responsible for the eventual fate of our world—individually and personally in small ways, universally and structurally in large ways.

Furthermore, Paul's Messianic/Christic revelation changed that end-time product into an in-time process with the metaphor of a harvest started and its first fruits already presented to God (1 Cor 15:12–13,16,20). Pharisaic faith was that, at least at end-time, the justice of God would be publicly revealed in a world finally and eternally justified. But, said Paul the Pharisee as a Messianic/Christic, that revelation had already started in-time as now-time with the Execution and Resurrection of Jesus. His Execution revealed a transcendental alternative to human wisdom. It disclosed a divine wisdom,

> not a wisdom of this age or of the rulers of this age, who are doomed to perish . . . [but] God's wisdom, secret and hidden, which God decreed before the ages for our glory. None of the rulers of this age understood this; for if they had, they would not have crucified the Lord of glory. (1 Cor 2:6–8)

For Paul, the Messianic/Christic Pharisee, the divine revelation of civilization's savage normalcy was that, "the god of this world" had not just killed "the glory of Christ, who is the image of God" (2 Cor 4:4) but had executed him publicly, officially, and—legally. On the one hand, then, what boast is left for law, what vaunt is left for civilization? On the other, what role is left—would have been left—for an uncrucified Messiah-Christ?

That transcendental tragedy had disclosed for Paul "the mystery that was kept secret for long ages" (Rom 16:25), namely, that, with civilization's official execution of the Messiah-Christ, universal resurrection, general judgment, and eternal sanctions were already present as now-time. They would not just happen at the end of time but were already—and always?—operational even if only revealed in now-time. Think of all that as both individual accountability and universal responsibility for our own creation of heaven versus hell as human options in this life rather than divine locations in the next.

Finally, throughout this book, when I use "Evolution," I am never simply referring to the negative evolution of Paul, Terror of the New Testament, from factual Pauline letters to fictional post-Pauline ones, from the Pauline-Paul to the Lukan-Paul and from Paul-versus-Peter to Peter-over-Paul. It was, however, necessary to follow that small-e evolution to establish the historical Paul whose revelation was a vision of post-civilization. This book had to work with the double-helix of Paul's historical DNA. It had to solve both the question of Paul's historical identity and raise the question of Paul's evolutionary relevance.

When, then, I use "Evolution" for the Fourth Matrix, it is as shorthand for Big-Bang-Evolution that created matter and energy, time and space, around fourteen billion years ago. Furthermore, when I meditate on Evolution, I see and can only see Evolution as a triadic vision of three-some in one-some, as a triple singularity, as triune Mystery not triune Person.

I formulate that triadic Mystery, for myself, as three questions that cannot be separated, three questions as one. They are, however, not questions for solution but questions for contemplation:

Why is there being rather than nothing?
Why is being dynamic rather than static?
Why is that dynamic just rather than unjust?

By "just," I mean that survival of the fittest is simply a transcendental redundancy for the unbiassed chance and equitable opportunity of all among all—from, say, volcano to virus, and parasite to person. Also, that triple oneness and especially that final justice is quite adequately *mysterium tremendum et fascinans*, a Mystery as terrifying as it is fascinating—for us.

The purpose of this book is to interpret Paul not simply through the cumulative matrices of Christian, Jewish, and Roman small histories—all of which must of course be recognized—but through the climactic matrix of Evolution as Big History. Whether, therefore, you read it as a committed theist, an impatient atheist, or an indifferent none, you—we—live together within Evolution and Paul's Pharisaic vision of universal responsibility and cosmic accountability in the now-time of his Messianic/Christic vision can best be described as an intuition of Evolution presented as a revelation of God.

Works Consulted

Agamben, Giorgio

> *The Time that Remains: A Commentary on the Letter to the Romans.* Trans. Patricia Dailey. Meridian Crossing Aesthetics. Ed. Werner Hamacher. Stanford, CA: Stanford University Press, 2005. Trans. from *Il tempo che resta: Un commento alla Lettera ai Romani.* Turin, Italy; Bollati Beringhieri, 2000.
> Epigraph of Chapter 9 is from pages 18, 67-68, & 75; of Chapter 10 is from pages 43 & 61; of Chapter 11 is from page 12.

Badiou, Alain

> *Saint Paul: The Foundation of Universalism.* Trans. Ray Brassier. Cultural Memory in the Present. Eds. Mieke Bal & Hent de Vries. Stanford, CA: Stanford University Press, 2003. Trans. From *Saint Paul: La fondation de l'universalisme.* Paris: Presses Universitaires de France, 1997. Epigraph of Chapter 4 is from page 17; of Chapter 7 is from pages 23-25.

Bowersock, Glen W.

> *Roman Arabia.* Cambridge, MA: Harvard University Press, 1983.
> Epigraph of Chapter 5 is from pages 45-65.

Gardner, W. H., & N. H. MacKenzie (Eds.)

> *The Poems of Gerard Manley Hopkins.* Fourth Edition, revised and enlarged. Oxford University Press, 1967.
> Epigraph of Prologue is from poem 101, page 142 (1864).

Taubes, Jacob

> *The Political Theology of Paul.* Eds. Aleida Assmann and Jan Assmann, in conjunction with Horst Folkers, Wolf-Daniel Hartwich, and Christoph Schulte. Trans. Dana Hollander. Cultural Memory in the Present. Eds. Mieke Bel and Hent de Vries. Stanford, CA: Stanford University Press, 2004. From *Lectures held at the Protestant Institute for Interdisciplinary Research (FEST) in Heidelberg, February 23-27, 1987.* Compiled on the basis of audio recordings by Aleida Assmann.
> Epigraph of Chapter 1 is from pages 5 & 11; of Chapter 3 is from pages 47-48; of Chapter 6 is from pages 19-20.

Made in the USA
Monee, IL
28 October 2024

68747550R00118